Tall Tales & Folderol
Balderdash & Tomfoolery
While Hunting Wild Turkeys

Shake A Tailfeather One More Time!

Tailfeather Press

After reviewing *Bend Over Shake a Tailfeather!* and *Bend Over Here It Comes!* the Press has concocted more Testimonials, Endorsements & Exaggerations:

"If you are all tied up with spur length and beard size, if your interest is in equipment and, 'Here I wuz and there he wuz and here is a picture of me with my foot on his neck,' then go somewhere else for your reading material. If you are interested in the intellectual process between man and turkey, and are willing to accept the fact that the turkey wins most of the time, then read Bill Privette. You are going to find some people in there that you know and a lot of people that think like you do." **Tom Kelly,** *The Tenth Legion,* **Wingfeather Press, Spanish Fort, Alabama**

"Bill's first book still is making me laugh when I think about his chapter on the anointing, when turkey droppings fell on him. His latest book covers more midsadventures while turkey hunting. The chapter on excuses will be helpful to hunters. It offers wild but believable explanations for missing a wild turkey. Bill loves to hunt wild turkeys and he has a wild sense of humor." **Jim Robey, Dayton Daily News, Dayton, Ohio**

"Bill is a minister by profession (retired) and a turkey hunter by passion. He is funny, irreverent (yep, a man of the cloth can earn this adjective) and a first-rate teller of tales. His first venture in books is an impressive one, full of good humor and all the craziness and calamities that are part of turkey hunting. Get his book and sample its pages. You'll find yourself coming back for more." **Jim Casada, Turkey & Turkey Hunting, Rock Hill, South Carolina**

"Bill isn't your ordinary turkey hunter. He's cut from a different piece of camouflage cloth than most people who carry a shotgun and wear a vest full of calls. He whets your appetite to go hunt these monarchs and tells his stories with a zany bit of genius that makes them fun to read.

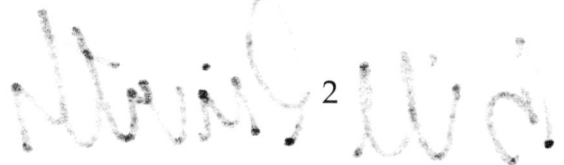

Hundreds of turkey-hunting books are out there. That said, I've read both of Bill's books. They are long on humor and hunters need something to laugh about once in a while. Privette is funny and serious, and that my friends, is a rare commodity among turkey hunters." **Dave Richey, DaveRichey.Com, Grawn, Michigan**

"Nearly all turkey hunters have a tale or two to tell, but can't or don't write them. Bill has more that a few tales to tell and he writes them masterfully with entertaining humor and wit. He has been around the turkey woods long enough to see just about everything imaginable and delightfully passes his tales on in this two "Bend Over" books. They both had me nodding with laughter and finding myself eager for the release of his third book in the trilogy. Keep them coming, Bill!" **Bobby "Doc" Dale,** *Double Gobble & Turkey Roost Tales,* **Tupelo, Mississippi.**

"I really enjoyed Bill's books. He is a talented professional and wrings the last bit of humor out of everything." **The late Wayne Bailey, Wayne's Turkey World: 60 Years of Hunting, Milton, North Carolina**

"Bill talks turkey with a sense of humor. He has learned to laugh at the silly mistakes, indignities and doses of humility doled out by Mother Nature. Even though the books are about turkey hunting, the experiences have universal appeal. Turkey wives love them because it is a voyeuristic look into what their husbands are into. Nonturkey hunters will like them because they are a combination of down-home philosophy and humor" **Chris Young, The Springfield Journal Register, Springfield, Illinois**

"Bill's books will make many hunters double over with laughter or bend over and shake a tailfeather. His writing style is similar to stories one would expect to hear around the campfire. All are well told, sometimes coarse, sometimes tender, oftentimes engrossing and always slapstick funny." **Jefferson Weaver, Bladen Journal, Elizabethtown, North Carolina**

"They say misery likes company. Privette, a noted outdoor writer, has traveled extensively in his quest for gobblers. His new book is long on self-deprecating humor, as are so many books telling tales of wild turkeys that always seem to hoodoo hunters." **Mike Marsh, Wilmington StarNews, Wilmington, North Carolina**

"Shake a Tailfeather is a great book for any hunter to read, you don't just have to be a turkey hunter to enjoy this lighthearted look at what it takes to sit for hours waiting for the big daddy bird to come into your shotgun sight. If you love a good laugh and want to learn the right and the wrong ways of turkey hunting, then this is the book for you. Or if you just want a look into Bill's life you won't be disappointed." **Randy Davey, Jacksonville Daily News, Jacksonville, North Carolina**

"I read Bill's books and almost laughed myself sick." Bill says, "This is not a good thing to do when one is long of tooth and short of breath." **Parker Whedon, Esquire, legendary NC turkey hunter, Charlotte, North Carolina**

Copyright © 2008 by William H. Privette
All rights reserved. No portion of this book may be reproduced or transmitted in any form or by any means, electronic or mechanical, including photocopying, recording or by any information storage and retrieval system, without written permission from the author, except for the inclusion of brief quotations in a review.
Photography and art are by the author unless otherwise attributed.

Published by Tailfeather Press
1119 Hendricks Avenue, Jacksonville, NC 28540.
www.TurkeyHuntBooks.Com

ISBN 10: 0-9777229-3-7
ISBN 13: 978-0-977722-93-8
September 2008

Library of Congress Control Number
2006906615

Privette, Bill
Shake A Tailfeather One More Time
Tall tales, folderal, balderdash and tom foolery while hunting wild turkeys.
1. Turkey Hunting – anecdotes, facetiae, satire
2. Outdoor Life – anecdotes, facetiae, satire

Printed in the United States by Morris Publishing
3212 East Highway 30
Kearney, NE 68847
1-800-650-7888

Pen and ink sketch courtesy of Phil Eddy, Dayton, Ohio.

Contents

Foreword & Memorial	8
Chapter One	13
Quickies	
Chapter Two	41
Peeping the Toms	
Chapter Three	53
Boinky Boink	
Chapter Four	61
Fall Fiasco	
Chapter Five	75
Return to Rose Brook	
Chapter Six	93
Creating Monsters	
Chapter Seven	109
Turkey Deja Vu	
Chapter Eight	117
Ghillie Suits & Seat Cushions	
Chapter Nine	129
Chester Departs Dodge	
Chapter Ten	141
The Power of Stink	
Chapter Eleven	155
Turkeys Don't	
Chapter Twelve	165
Win Without a Fight	
Chapter Thirteen	175
One Below	
Chapter Fourteen	193
Turkey Lounger For Sale	

Foreword & Memorial

"Uncle" Doug Jackson on the Ausable River,
Michigan, May 1988
August 1, 1948 – April 15, 2008

It is with a heavy heart that I dedicate this book to my recently departed brother-in-law, Doug Jackson. Doug died unexpectedly from pancreatic cancer, after just three and a half weeks in the hospital. The cancer had spread to lungs, liver and spine and chemotherapy offered little hope. Showing great courage, devout faith and trust in God, he refused the treatment. He died four days later. He was 59 years old.

Although I could not convert Doug to the one true religion, turkey hunting, he did give it a half-hearted try or two. I believe his first turkey hunt was at Rose Brook Farm on opening day in Missouri, many years ago. I don't remember the year. I had persuaded him to drive up to Illinois from Wilmington, North Carolina, as I had talked him into many such hunting and fishing trips over four decades. It rained the whole time, torrential downpours. We did not shoot a turkey.

One of my favorite adventures included a quality trip to the famous Ausable River in Grayling, Michigan in 1988. My oldest son, Heath, who was 14 years old at the time, went with us and, most importantly, it did not rain! And we caught fish!!

We fished the famous South Branch and caught and released native brook trout. I took the photo of Doug, on the opposite page, on the Main Branch of the river, just down from Rusty Gates' lodge. That morning I spent most of my time tying black caddis flies, supplying the boys with the fly *du jour* – the only fly that the trout preferred to hit. I sat at my fly bench in the motel room, as fast as I could tie them, the boys would dash in from the river, grab up the flies, and head back out.

I met Doug almost 40 years ago. He was a tall, skinny fellow – 6 feet, 8 inches - with thick, curly hair and a great sense of humor. He drove a vintage blue Volkswagen beetle and dated my wife's sister at Duke University. He had graduated from UNC Wilmington the year before and would drive up to Duke on the weekends and stay with me. My wife, who was at Salem College in Winston-Salem at the time, would come down and stay with her sister and we would double date all weekend. I had a single room at the time and kept a seven-foot mattress tucked under my bed for use on the weekends. Thus, Doug became my unofficial roommate that year in college.

Susan graduated from Duke in May and they got married in August 1971. Karen and I got married the following May, after I graduated. After we settled in to married life, I introduced Doug to the fine art of fly-fishing AND the pursuit of ducks, quail and other feathered fowl. To make a 40-year story short, we chased trout, bass, flounder, quail, ducks, geese, grouse, pheasant and, yes, even wild turkeys all over the United States.

Since Doug and Susan did not have any children, I made sure that my children, especially my two sons, spent as much time with their uncle as they could. They were able to hunt and fish with Doug and me, again, all over the country. And they loved every minute! Moreover, they are better young men for it.

I could fill the pages of several books with Bill and Doug stories and maybe one day I will do just that. For the time being, suffice it to say, I have reached a milestone in my life where I join the exclusive company of others who have lost a very special outdoor companion. In addition, I have lost a big brother, a best friend and my Number One reader/fan. If ever there was one, Doug was the epitome of the loyal, dependable and encouraging companion in the complete journey of life.

I feel a great empty space in my life now where Doug used to be. He is gone and we will no longer share hunting and fishing trips, oyster roasts, wild game dinners, new movies to see, new books to read or weekly phone calls to catch up. With time, my grief will diminish. It always does. I also know that no one will fill Doug's position either.

Doug Jackson was a once-in-a-life gift to all of us who knew and loved him so dearly. I was awful lucky to have him for 40 years. I will remember him each day and cherish our time together. For the rest of my life. That will be enough to tide me over. ↓↓

Tom Crook's remote game camera took this photo on Sunday, while Tom was in church! Bobby Dale sent this to me.

Chapter One

"Quickies"
Wham, Bam, Thank You, Ma'am

Every now and then, even a blind hog will find an acorn, and every now and then a fortuitous turkey hunter will bag a gobbler right off the roost. These hunts tend to be few and far between, but they also tend to be the most memorable. If you have hunted for any amount of time – 10, 15, 20 years or longer – you will have been fortunate enough to garner enough of these quickie hunts under your belt to keep you honest, appreciative and otherwise spoiled.

For the purpose of this chapter, I would like to recall and exposit three or four of these more exceptional and expeditious hunts. Naturally I will have to exaggerate, prevaricate, postulate and prolongate in order to lengthen the story and fill enough pages as necessary to keep the printer happy and paid. Since these hunts were brief, lasting only minutes, I could recount them using very few words and little paper. Which I had to do on a consistent basis back in my newspaper days.

On the other hand, just because they were in and of themselves quick hunts does not mean that I have to be terse or sparse in my recollections. On the contrary, the opportunity to expand upon all sorts and conditions of observations will present itself in due course.

Forsooth, let us begin with the dispatching of the county record longbeard residing on Gobbler Knob at Rose Brook Farm, Clopton, Missouri.

As I have mentioned in earlier accounts, this particular longbeard had eluded me on an earlier hunt. I had positioned myself down in the creek bottom below the roosting bird in a lovely spot, picturesque and pleasant to view. I had piled up some dead logs and limbs on an earlier outing to construct a rather adequate blind and found myself sitting there often as the first light of morning bathed the landscape around me.

On more than one occasion, I sat in this rustic blind and fantasized that I had bought this particular piece of land and it was all mine. Down the creek to the east, about a half-mile or so, my dream log home stood, with wide porches and stone fireplaces. All I had to do to hunt spring and fall turkeys was pick up my gear and gun, walk out my back door and hike up the creek. It would take winning the Power Ball lottery to make this dream come true. But, something tells me my ship ain't gonna come in. It sank a long time ago.

It was and still is a most beautiful hollow, the most marvelous hardwood valley in the whole state of Missouri. The valley is nestled between two large hills and features a small brook meandering through the spacious bottomland middle, with a winding old log road by its side. In western parlance, you would call it a box canyon because the west side of the hollow ends and rises to a long saddle ridge that joins the two knobs. The east side of the valley flows into a large pasture, owned by the neighboring farmer.

The hollow features a generous number of mature oak trees, acorn laden and spread out in such a grand fashion that the hunter can sit quietly in a natural blind (a stack of dead limbs and fresh cut leafy branches) and simply watch the woods come alive with all sorts and conditions of wild critters, far and wide.

To the south, Gobbler Knob towers above the valley floor and provides the turkey hunter with many opportunities to roost and kill fat Missouri longbeards. To the north, Hammer Knob ascends and renders more roosting gobblers, including the infamous Hammer, itself. On many a spring and fall morning, when I did not know exactly where birds were to be found, I would slip into the Back Valley and settle into my blind and wait for something to happen. And, it always did.

On this particular morning, my buddy, Doc Lucky, accompanied me. In fact, I think it was only his second or third hunt at Rose Brook. We had roosted the big bird on Gobbler Knob the evening before simply by driving up to the top of the gap between Fifteen Gobbler Knob and Hammer Knob, getting out of the Jeep and listening at sunset. The big bird obliged us with several lusty gobbles before it flew up to roost.

When we arrived early the next morning in the dark, I knew exactly what to do and where to go. Instead of sneaking into the blind in the bottom, we crossed the creek and hiked up Gobbler Knob, using a well-worn deer trail that snaked up the west side of the knob and away from the gobbling bird. We moved quickly and quietly because we had no time to waste.

Just as we crossed the creek and began our ascent, the big tom bellowed out its first gobble from above and it echoed in the hollow below. The tom continued to gobble steadily as we advanced up the steep side of the knob at a fast pace. When we finally arrived at the top, we had reached two benches, two narrow but flat terraces that stretched along the west side of the knob. Two perfect places to sit down and get ready. Thanks to the steady gobbling and the almost full foliage in the trees, we were able to sneak into place not more than 50 yards away from the loud tom.

Our approach had been flawless. Fast, silent and ending in the perfect set-up spot. I pointed to a good spot next to a large oak where Doc needed to sit in order to cover the lower bench in case the tom flew down and landed there. I climbed a few more steps up and settled into a dead tree on the ground. I could see the upper bench completely and part of the top of the knob, too. All the while, the longbeard gobbled intensely. And close by.

Dripping with sweat, my glasses fogged up from the vapor. I took a deep breath, relaxed, wiped off my glasses and slipped out my slate call from my vest. When the right moment arrived, I softly scratched three or four tantalizing yelps to the gobbler, which zeroed in on the call and went silent. A minute later, not much more than that, I heard the big bird launch from the tree, feathers beating loudly against the new leaves. Then I saw it descend to the ground in a great flurry of wings back peddling the air, on the upper bench, my bench.

I proceeded to aim the Eliminator, my 11-87 SPS, with its brand new scope, in the direction of the gobbler. At the same time, I hit the bird with loud cutts and yelps from my Quaker Boy Split Quad. My glasses fogged up again and I slowly wiped the lenses clear while they were perched on my nose with my glove finger. The big tom double-gobbled back at my calls;

hunched over and made a beeline in my direction.

I tracked the bird through my scope and studied its size, beard and spurs. It was indeed a dandy, a big'un. Twenty-five yards out, it slipped under a dead tree, leaning at a 45-degree angle, and appeared on my side. I pushed the safety button off and took a deep breath. The tom continued to walk slowly in my direction, head erect and eyes scouring the terrain for the hen that had announced its presence so close by. I hunkered down into the limbs of the dead tree and let my breath out slowly.

The crosshairs on my scope dissected the turkey at the base of the neck. I steadied my aim and pulled the trigger.

Ka-blam!

The big gobbler collapsed. A couple of wing flops ensued and the bird was out for the count. When I stood up, I noticed another tom scurrying away down the backside of the hill. There were two birds on Gobbler Knob. If I had known that fact, in the first place, I would have sat still and tried to call in the second bird for Jeff to shoot, in the second place. But, obviously, I did not. Sorry, Jeff.

Normally, when you have two longbeards together, the dominant bird will hang back and let the subdominant bird take the lead. That way if danger is ahead the subdominant will take one for the team. Howsumever, in this case, the big bird arrived first and I dispatched it summarily and without delay. We did not have time to get acquainted nor did I give it a name. I just shot it.

It weighed just a couple of ounces shy of 26 pounds. It had a 12-inch beard and almost 2-inch spurs. I noticed the weight as soon as I picked it up and slung it over my shoulder. It was the heaviest turkey I had ever shot. And I had to carry out of the woods. By the time we got back to the truck, it weighed 50 pounds. Jeff arrived and was speechless.

Impressed was an understatement. It was the largest turkey he had ever seen!

I tried to talk him into carrying it back to the truck for me. But he would not oblige. He just smiled and said, "You shot it. You carry it." And I did. He did carry my shotgun because it took both hands to hold on to the fat tom and I had to stop several times to catch my breath and rest my arms.

From the time we arrived on top of Gobbler Knob until the time I shot, about five minutes had elapsed. Maybe less, but definitely not more.

We hiked down the knob and up the next hill to my Jeep. From the time we left the Jeep and returned, 30 minutes had passed. The gobbler also weighed about 40 pounds. Although this hunt was brief, it was not my shortest one.

Another memorable quickie hunt occurred in Cass County, Illinois, when the local weatherman had predicted a nasty storm front approaching Springfield from the southwest.

We're talking wind, hail, thunder and lightning. Did I mention that I did not particularly care for lightning, especially if I am sitting out in the open on the edge of a field waiting for a turkey to show up?

Well, I almost let the weatherman talk me out of the hunt that morning. Then I remembered other mornings when I stayed home, expecting bad weather, and the weatherman was wrong. So, I figured what the heck? I had one more Illinois tag to fill so I would set the alarm and get up no matter what. I would check the weather after I had awakened and then decide to go or stay home and shoot turkeys in my dreams.

I woke up the next morning five minutes before the alarm went off. As usual. I slipped into my hunting clothes and left the bedroom quietly without waking my wife. When I got downstairs, I opened the front door and walked out into the front yard. Above me, a Midwest sky filled with bright twinkling stars greeted me. Screw you, Mr. Weatherman.

I left my house with time to spare and drove west out of town towards Cass County. All the way out to the Upper 125 farm, near Beardstown, the wide-open prairie sky twinkled with millions of stars. Absolutely no hint of a storm front was in sight. It took 45 minutes to reach the farm but the drive was always worth it. The Upper 125 farm had furnished me with at least two spring longbeards and one fall tom for five or six years in a row. I would have driven ten hours and 45 minutes to get to it and hunt.

The first time I saw the Upper 125 farm, I was not impressed. Bill Pittman's brother-in-law, Peter Arnold, had met Bill, Mark and Trudy Faull and me one Sunday afternoon and showed off the farm. The farm featured several pastures, small, medium and large, carved out of the Illinois River bluffs. There were absolutely no hardwoods on the property. Just pastures, electric fences and a small herd of cows. The black and white jobbies.

Peter was from Switzerland and farmed this land and two other farms with his brother and father. They raised hogs on the other farms but they grazed cattle on the Upper 125. Their technique for hog farming and cattle ranching is worth mentioning before I move on.

The Arnolds used portable electric fences to restrict the livestock to a small area of a pasture. When that area was thoroughly grazed, they moved the electric fences. Most American farmers, from my experience, won't spend that much time and energy moving fences. The Swiss obviously have a different standard of farming. Clean and efficient. Imagine a hog farm that does not stink. T'is true.

Anyway, I did not say anything as we toured the farm and surveyed the pastures with Peter. I was happy to have permission to hunt a private farm and figured a turkey or two might show up every once and awhile. But, the hardwoods that surrounded the farm and belonged to the neighbors looked awesome and probably held most of the turkeys.

Was I ever wrong! And happy to admit it!

I had absolutely and totally no idea, no clue, no intimation that Peter was showing us the Grand Central Station of Strut, the Sacred Shrine of Spit, the Delirious Delta of Drum, the most heavily visited strut zone in the whole wide world!

Turkeys all over Cass County, from far and wide, top and bottom, made their spring pilgrimage to the long, narrow pasture at the top of the bluff to strut their stuff. They took numbers, stood in line and waited for their turn to strut out onto the pasture and shake their tail feathers. I am not exaggerating! It was too good to be true. But, it was true.

Well, back to the story. I arrived at the fabulous farm of fowl, the plentitudinous plantation of poultry, the grandiose grange of gobblers, with plenty of time to spare and drove up the winding dirt road to the top pasture. I parked at the last curve and silently geared up and left the Jeep. I hiked the final stretch of road and entered the pasture in the dark. The stars overhead continued to shine on me. No sign of a severe storm front anywhere. Go figure.

I quickly walked about halfway down the east side of the pasture and parked my frame down beside a massive oak tree. One of those classic Midwestern sentinel oaks that was at least 150 years old, maybe older. I had shot several turkeys while sitting against the tree and figured one more longbeard would not be asking too much.

Before long, a gobbler cranked up in the neighbor's woodlot behind me and about 100 yards away. I waited about 10 minutes and finally greeted the bird with some choice soft seductive yelps. Two, maybe three. The gobbler went silent, then gobbled again. The next thing I knew, I heard the bird fly down and, voila, it appeared from the woods and began to strut in the pasture about 100 yards to my left.

As I watched the tom strut and called to it, the sky began to lighten and, lo and behold, a massive line of dark, foreboding clouds appeared low on the western horizon. The wind picked up and blew from the direction of the storm clouds. The predicted storm front was on its way. I could smell the rain coming.

I checked my watch and figured I had about 20 minutes maximum before the storm arrived. I checked the tom and it was taking its time coming my way. I revved my calling up another notch. I figured I had less than 15 minutes to shoot this turkey and get back to the Jeep before all heck broke loose.

The hot calling fired up the tom and five minutes later the bird arrived 35 yards away. I aimed the crosshairs of my scope on the base of its neck and pulled the trigger.

Whammm!

The bird flipped over and lay flat on its back, wings slapping the air and legs pumping the invisible bicycle.

With no time to waste, I jumped up, snatched my decoy and stuffed it into my vest back pocket. I grabbed the flopping tom, flung it over my shoulder – still flopping - and trotted to the Jeep. When I arrived at the vehicle, I popped open the tailgate, tossed in the tom, inspected the spurs and beard – a nice three-year-old bird – and slammed the tailgate shut.

By this time, the wind had picked up and was blowing strong. The storm front had arrived and big drops of rain splattered on the road and Jeep. I jumped behind the wheel, cranked the engine and headed home. As I drove down the hill to the highway, a bolt of lightning split the sky, followed by a booming peal of thunder.

The weatherman was correct after all. A large and violent storm front had arrived and I was in the middle of it. But, this time it did not mess up my turkey hunt. I figured from the time I left my Jeep, sat down by the oak tree, and shot the bird, it took maybe 15 to 20 minutes. That was all the time I had before the storm arrived and ruined everything. Not to mention me sitting by a big lightning rod oak tree and getting zapped by Zeus. Talk about shooting a turkey just in the nick of time.

I felt pretty satisfied as I drove the 45-minutes back home. I stayed just ahead of the storm and arrived home safely 10 minutes ahead of the tempest. I pulled into the garage, out of the wind and rain, and inspected my longbeard more closely. Yep, I had done good. It was a dandy.

The time was 6:45 a.m. I still had time to cook breakfast, shower, drop the bird by Tim's deli, deposit it in his walk-in freezer and head to the office. What a great way to start the business day!

The bird weighed 22 pounds, had an 11-inch beard and one-and-a-quarter-inch spurs. It was my fourth longbeard that spring and I still had two New York tags to fill. Which I proceeded to accomplish.

My most favorite quickie hunt features the Back Valley at Rose Brook Farm once again and outsmarting my Missouri nemesis, the Goober.

For many, many years, I had Rose Brook all to myself. I would hunt there alone quite often. Sometimes I would bring a friend. On the back side of Hammer Knob was a beautiful valley with a small creek meandering through the middle. The woods were wide open and stately oak trees stood guard with timeless grace. I had built a most comfortable and suitable blind from dead limbs and brush in this valley. Up against one of those sentinel oaks, I have spent many a blissful hour, sitting in the blind and shutting out the chaotic world beyond. Before I retired, turkey hunting was a most effective way for me to block out the constant stress of work and obligations.

On one fine fall afternoon, I was contently yelping away on my slate in the blind when a young gobbler answered my calls. Its yelps were deep and coarse, but they possessed that plaintive resonance, which we come to recognize from experience, as a young gobbler's voice. I put the call down and raised my shotgun in the direction of the gobbler.

When there should have been silence and then a bird appearing next to and down the creek, another set of yelps broke forth instead. I realized in a second that my young gobbler was none other than the Goober – the new hunter who had violated my valley from the neighbor's farm to the south the previous spring.

Before long, I spotted movement and it did not belong to a turkey. It was the Goober, slicing away on a box call as he walked up the creek valley. One hundred yards away. He was doing a good job at whacking the box and he had fooled me at first. But, I had finally heard the telltale squeak of the paddle screw on the last series of calls and knew it was not a turkey.

Since I was, for all intent and purpose, trapped in the blind, I hunkered down and hid. The Goober continued in my direction but veered off at the last minute and trudged up the hill on the other side of the creek. Fortuitously, he did not get close enough to see the blind and me.

With this encounter lodged in my memory, I slipped into the valley the very next spring on opening day of the Missouri season. Since I had arrived at the farm too late on the evening before to roost a bird, I figured I would slip quietly in the dark to the blind, sit and wait for the turkey world to wake up. Chances were that several old gobblers were roosting in the valley and would make their way down the creek and to me, sooner or later.

I will never forget my mood that morning. I did not have a care in the world. There I was, sitting in the pile of logs and branches I had arranged into a natural blind. I relaxed and dozed on and off. It was opening day of turkey season in Missouri and I was sitting in the back valley. I was the luckiest man alive and wallowing, like a fat hog in the mud, in deep contentment.

Dawn arrived with the gray light of early morning filling the valley. A couple of barred owls hooted far in the distance. The robins woke up and chattered in the woods around me. The cardinals whistled their *"pretty-pretty"* mating calls from the brush. And, as more light bathed the tall stately oak trees, a gobble erupted about 100 yards behind me and up the backside of Hammer Knob.

Now this was unusual. A complete and total surprise.

In my ten years of hunting in the valley, not once had a spring gobbler roosted on the backside of Hammer Knob. Not once. No sir. I was pleasantly surprised, to say the least, to hear one gobbling there but I did not worry. I turned around in the blind, faced the direction of the love call, rested the shotgun on a log and waited to respond. It was just a tad early.

Ten minutes later, another gobble burst forth. A loud, lusty one announcing the opening of spring turkey season. I waited a minute, composed myself and then responded with three soft yelps from my little Jet slate. I waited again. I could picture the old bird, cocking its head in my direction and triangulating my location.

The silence was golden and I waited contently. I might just get this old bird to come down to me, I told myself.

My thoughts were interrupted when a box call crank up way down the creek. Ye Gads! It was the Goober. I could not help but recognize the onerous box this time. My stomach flipped and I felt a sickness envelope me. The infirmity was none other than the demon, Dread. Deep and dark and foreboding. The Goober was headed my way and bound to screw things up. Once again.

Immediately, I began to send ESP messages to the Hammer Knob gobbler to shut the heck up. One more gobble and the Goober would come running. Trouble rides a fast horse.

I began to calculate as best I could the time and distance formula between the Goober and me. As best I could reckon, I had about 10 minutes, maybe 15 in a pinch, before he arrived and ruined the hunt. That is if the old gobbler received my message and kept its mouth shut.

On the other hand, I could not bank on the turkey staying quiet so I needed to speed things up, if I could. I took the risk.

Now, hindsight being 20-20 and Uncas being the last Mohican, if I had had me one of my sweet talking wing bone yelpers, it would not have been much of a risk. A couple of seductive, soft yelps on the bone and that gobbler would have come a running. But, alas, I did not make them back in those days nor knew much about the seductive power of wing bones.

Instead, I produced my well-worn little Lynch Jet Slate and tenderly stroked three dulcet notes, punctuated with a gentle cluck at the end. Three mellifluous yelps wafted up through the treetops. I put the call back in my pocket and waited. The old bird got my message.

Almost immediately, I heard loud wing beats explode from the hill above and soon I witnessed the old gobbler flying down and landing 50 yards from me. I slowly raised my gun and tracked the bird as it waltzed straight for me. At 35 yards, my trigger finger lingered a few seconds while I admired its long beard and full fan. Completely satisfied, I commenced to squeeze the trigger.

Ka-blammo! The longbeard hit the deck stone dead.

The shot shattered the peaceful valley and reverberated off the hillsides. I am sure the Goober, who was still a good distance down the creek, heard the shot. However, with all the echoes ricocheting off the hillsides, there was no way he could pinpoint where it had come from or determine exactly what had happened. Furthermore, I did not want him to know exactly what had happened, lest he camp out on Hammer Knob for the rest of the spring season. As fast as greased lightning, I proceeded to jump up, run up the hill, police up the loose feathers, grab the old gobbler by the legs and head back to the Jeep.

I felt pretty darn sassy with myself as I summarily and furtively vacated the premises. Elvis had left the building! With a fat old gobbler in tow. Soup for Brains Goober did not have a clue. Art had taught me this useful trick many years earlier and I had remembered to use it one more time. Keep the other hunters guessing. Divulge a minimum of information. Leave no clues behind. Stealth turkey hunting at its best.

Not only did I dispatch a dandy longbeard, right off the bat, on opening day. But, right out from under the nose of the good old worthless Goober. Not too shabby. And the Goober was left holding an empty bag, which he deserved to tote, and a puzzle he will never solve, unless he reads this story. And, I have my doubts that he will.

The previous spring, the Goober had busted into a hot tom that Big Doug and I had coming to the gun. I had feared the same fate again. This time, however, the worm had turned.

The hunt, if you count the minutes from the first gobble to the shot, took 10 minutes, more or less. This was cutting things pretty close, if I were going to keep the Goober out of the picture.

On several, more occasions that particular spring, I tried to intercept and meet His Gooberness in the back valley. I figured my best bet was to make his acquaintance and help him keep out of my way. I was unsuccessful. I did dispatch my second Missouri tom that spring but not in the back valley. I caught that old gobbler with two jakes and a hen on the west side of Hammer Knob. I killed this old gobbler using fall tactics. Another story, another time.

Another all-time swifty-nifty hunt was the time Art and I hunted spring birds in Hodge Gulf, Chautauqua County, New York. I forget the year.

My job back in those early apprentice days was to go out in the evening and roost birds while Art did chores – cut the grass, split wood or work up at the farm. This was easy choice to make, if you have half the sense God gave an ant.

"Oh please, Brer Fox, whatever you do, don't throw me into the briar patch," said Brer Rabbit.

"I just hate watching turkeys, Brer Fox. I'd rather cut crass, split wood and fill out my tax forms. Please don't make me go roost turkeys!"

On one such lovely spring evening, I drove the Jeep down the truck trail (forest service road) to Hodge Gulf, parked and plucked myself in a good listening spot and commenced to pay close attention. At sunset, 8 o'clock on the dot, the VFD siren blasted in Gerry. And, several gobblers shock gobbled in response to the blast. They were roosting directly across from me on the opposite hillside above the creek. I selected a gnarly old dead tree as my landmark and proceeded to head back to the village. Whereupon, I reported to Brer Fox, the Chief Turkey Hunter, himself, that I was successful in finding the next morning's quarry.

We settled in that evening to watch homemade turkey videos and eat supper. Art fell asleep in his Lazy Boy recliner. I slipped quietly upstairs and into bed. I was so tired that night that I thanked the Lord for dividing two days with one night. I fell asleep as fast as a tuckered out bird dog in front of a cozy warm fireplace.

Art awoke early the next morning and puttered around in the kitchen. About 4:30 a.m., he flicked the stairwell light on and off and announced it was time for me to wake up. Which I did. After visiting the bathroom, I quickly slipped into my hunting clothes and headed for the kitchen for a hot cup of coffee and some Little Debbie jellyrolls.

We proceeded to load up the truck and in due time pulled out of the village and headed for Hodge Gulf and a rendezvous with the gobblers who slept there. We arrived and parked quietly at the turnaround. Quickly, we geared up, walked down the road and sneaked over to the gnarly dead tree. We proceeded to sit down, with me about 20 yards down the hill and in front of Art. We waited for the sun to rise.

Before long, the opposing hillside rocked and rolled, shaked and rattled, with gobbles. From the count, we figured at least four birds, maybe five, were roosting in the trees and were taking turns gobbling. They put on quite a show, a gobble fest that I won't easily forget. The gobbles tumbled like dominos, non-stop, for 20 minutes.

Finally, Art was able to get a yelp or two in edgewise. Just one hearty yelp, maybe two and no more calls. Then silence.

I could picture those birds cocking their heads and zeroing in on Art's location, 20 yards directly behind me. Seconds later the cool, calm morning reverberated with multitudinous wing beats, growing louder as the birds launched one by one and headed right for us. A lusty gobble announced their arrival at the foot of the hill below me. I raised my Winchester 1300 and held my aim steady.

Voila! A big old white noggin, the size of a softball, sporting blue cheeks, red wattles and two beady eyes, appeared below me and at the end of my gun barrel. Ten yards away. I started to squeeze the trigger but stopped.

Another big white head popped up beside the first one! And behind it, the third gobbler head stuck up. I had three old gobblers lined up as pretty as a picture. If I shot the first one, all three would tumble. The thought flirted across my mind. I was sorely tempted. But, I passed the shot. One gobbler per day in New York. Period.

A second later, the first old gobbler took a step sideways and raised its head. Clear.

Kabaaaam! The 1300 roared and the turkey flipped over doornail dead. The other birds exploded into the air and departed the scene post haste.

It has been awhile since I have had three gobblers lined up for one shot. The most recent time was in Cass County, when I called in four old toms, side by side, for Doc Lucky and me to dispatch. Again, legally. One a piece. It is a rare gift indeed to behold such a sight. Rare and quite marvelous.

If I had to pick a critical ingredient to quick hunts, it would be to be there the "firstest with the mostest" – a Civil War general said this – Nathan Bedford Forest. Most of my quickie hunts were on private land and no competition or interference messed up the Mojo. It was easier to call green birds, as it were, and coaxed them in quickly. Soft, seductive and sparse calling was all that was really needed.

The right set up was and still is critical. I needed to be in a hot spot, with good visibility, shooting lanes and good cover. Decent weather helped a lot, also.

And, lest we forget the most important ingredient. A thick slice of good old-fashioned Mojo was a definite plus. Two surefire Mojo motivators include holding your butt cheeks just right and wearing clean underwear. Sprinkling the blood of a dead turkey on your head at midnight in the Garden of Good and Evil will help, too.

Finally, this deserves a second mention. Quickie hunts are few and far between. Do not get the idea that they happen all the time. Just because you see a 20-minute turkey hunt on TV does not mean that your hunts will last 20 minutes or less. Ninety-nine percent of your hunts will take hours, if not days.

If, on the other hand, you are lucky enough to experience a quickie hunt, every now or then, savor the moment. It may be two or three years later before you pass that way again. Maybe even longer!

Finally, I need to include a very special quickie hunt, "the lap turkey" hunt. Lap turkeys are as rare as politicians that do not lie. And we know they are lying because their lips are moving. During my quarter-century plus of chasing wild turkeys, I have experienced only one lap turkey hunt. I have heard about these hunts from other hunters but I have experienced only one in my life. So far.

I was most fortunate to return to Rose Brook Farm, near Eolia, Missouri, during a recent spring season and on the third morning of my hunt, whilst I was working on bird Number Two; I was bestowed with the rare gift of a lap turkey. My good friend and author, Bobby Dale, had traveled up from Tupelo, Mississippi to hunt with me for a few days. This was Bobby's first visit to Missouri and I was delighted to have him with me.

That particular morning I sent Bobby off to the Back Valley to chase several vocal gobblers that resided there. I headed for Black's Field, the back end, where I had erected my blind a few days earlier and bumped off a dandy longbeard the first day of my hunt. My plan was simple. I would hole up in my blind, call sporadically, and read Andy Adams's book, *The Log of a Cowboy*, written in 1903.

I need to mention the fact that by the time I arrived in Missouri I had given up "running and gunning" for gobblers for good. A three-foot Copperhead that slowly slithered out from under my Gobbler Lounger seat and in between my legs the previous week in North Carolina had convinced me that sitting on the ground was not a good idea. Another story, another time.

After I arrived at my blind, on that cloudy, damp, pre-dawn morning, I lit my pipe and puffed quietly whilst waiting for gobbling in the woods nearby. At first light, a bird announced its presence, halfway up a nearby knob, with a lusty gobble that signaled a mature longbeard. As I had encountered other birds in the past, roosting on that knob, and had had these birds ignore my calls, fly down and travel up the knob and away from me, I decided that my blind was close enough to the bird, so I got inside, sat down and waited.

I figured the gobbler would eventually fly down, go silent and maybe show up in the field later in the morning. After all, that was what had happened to me in the past, including the most recent hunt, two days earlier. On that morning, a bird gobbled profusely not far away in the woods and, four hours later, it appeared in the field in shotgun range. I whacked that bird at about 45 yards. Forsooth, I assumed that déjà vu, all over again, was my best bet for taking bird Number Two.

This particular tom gobbled, as I described to Bobby later, "excessively". It gobbled over and over, sometimes facing me, sometimes facing the other direction. When the crows cranked up, about 15 minutes or so before sunrise - I don't usually wear a watch and tell time by nature - I decided to share some "Sweetness" on the gobbling tom. I slipped out my Lynch Jet Slate, sanded the small stone surface and scratched the sweetest clucks and tree yelps you have ever heard. Mr. Excessive Gobbler shut right up.

Which is good. The silence meant that the gobbler had heard me and probably was craning its neck so its ears could zero in on the exact location of the hen that had yelped. I waited.

It wasn't long before the gobbler blasted a lusty gobble right at me and I immediately knew that my dose of "Sweetness" had done the trick. Although many turkey hunters would have answered right back, I knew better. I responded with a heavy dose of silence. The gobbler went crazy and continued to gobble its head off, directly at me.

By now, the back end of the pasture was showing the first signs of sunlight. I figured it was close to fly-down time and I might as well pull out the cowboy book and start reading. The gobbler was going to fly down, shut up and strut its tail feathers up the knob and away from me. So, I rustled around in my vest, looking for the book.

When all of a sudden I heard loud wing beats, coming DOWN from the knob.

I looked up and, lo and behold, right smack dab in front of me, the excessive gobbling gobbler landed with a flurry of back-peddling wings. Practically right in my lap.

Fortunately, I was well hidden inside my blind and was able to shoulder my shotgun and line up the shot without the longbeard seeing a thing. The bird stood at regal attention, surveying the pasture and my Bobble Head hen decoy. I smoothly placed the sight's red dot on the base of the gobbler's neck and squeezed the trigger.

Whammmmo! The gobbler collapsed and did not move. Gobble, gobble, no more. My hunt was over.

When I got back to the truck, I checked the time on the dashboard radio. 6:00 a.m. Not only had I accomplished another wham-bam-thank-you-ma'am hunt but also it included the elusive, rare and extraordinary "lap turkey".

If I never get to turkey hunt again, I will go to the bone yard content with the sweet memory of my lap turkey. The Hole in One of turkey hunting.

The longbeard turned out to be a 24-pound, two-year old. A couple of days later, my daughter baked the breasts in her famous turkey potpie. The tail fan, beard and spurs are special artifacts in my wild turkey collection. I spent the rest of the morning, sitting in my truck, reading the cowboy book and waiting for Bobby to come out of the Back Valley. The wind turned cold. The rain spattered non-stop on my windshield. Another fine and miserable spring morning in eastern Missouri passed on by.

It was time to head for Illinois and hunt in Cass County. ↓↓

Eight gobblers strut their stuff on a farm near the White Oak River, Onslow County, North Carolina. I was lucky enough to bump off one of them when the hunting season arrived later.

Chapter Two

"Scouting"
Peeping the Toms

True confession time. I love to watch wild turkeys – fall, winter, spring and summer. Morning, noon and night. I find them absolutely fascinating and I learn something new almost every time I watch them. Some hunters call turkey watching, "scouting". I call it fun. Since we cannot hunt turkeys like the old-timers used to – in the fall and winter with a three-month season – we can still watch them. No matter the season.

The more I watch turkeys, the more I figure them out and the better hunter I inevitably become. Remembering, however, what Art Kibbe says, "The only thing predictable about turkeys is that they are unpredictable." Thus, I watch turkeys in order to understand more about their behavior but I also season those observations with a generous portion of unpredictability.

When I go scouting, I usually carry with me a camera or two, video and SLR, and a strong pair of field glasses, 10X or better. Dan Kibbe gave his dad, Art, a super high-powered spotting scope for Christmas one year. I forget the power but it was reach-out-there-and-touch-someone telescopic. We clipped it to the truck window and spent several evenings watching old gobblers strut on "Sunny Side" while we parked in the high school parking lot. I was easily entertained in those days. Still am. Art, too.

Moreover, this is as good a place as any to mention that it takes a hard-core, super-committed turkey hunter to watch homemade turkey videos. I know of only two persons that fit this bill. Art and me. We can watch homemade videos for hours upon hours. We might doze a little in the middle, but as far as I can recall, we are the only two turkey hunters that I know who can watch those jumpy, jerky, "oops I dropped the camera" videos from start to finish. And, most of all, appreciate them! Warts and all. Makes no difference. They are all Academy Award winners.

I have quite a collection now of VHS and 8mm tapes. However, Art holds the record. He has an extensive, expansive and otherwise enormous collection of hundreds of 8mm turkey tapes. He has burned up two Sony camcorders in the process of stockpiling this footage. I tried to explain to Art, while on our third trip to the camera repair shop in Jamestown, that his video camera was designed to work for an average number of hours. Moreover, that he had far exceeded those hours during the first six months of ownership.

At any rate, Art continues to tape turkeys and all sorts of wild critters, day in and day out. One of these days, hopefully in the far off future, his grand children will have a wonderful library of wildlife videos produced by their grandfather. Let us hope that they will appreciate the tremendous gift that it is. As for my own kids and their kids, they could give a rodent's rectum about my tapes. When they were still living at home and getting on my nerves, I would pop one of those tapes into the VCR and the room would clear out so fast you would have thought someone had passed terrible gas. I know who is going to get my tapes when I am ten toes up and six feet under. Art!

Forsooth, turkey scouting not only includes turkey watching but turkey photography as well. I have yet to invest in one of those new fandangled digital cameras that you strap on a tree, leave out in the woods and catch critters creeping by. The price tag is still too deep for my shallow pockets. Plus, it rather takes the fun out of watching the woods, first hand. Defeats the purpose, as it were, of bird watching.

Back to turkey watching first-hand. When I first began turkey hunting, the Ohio season was short, just a week or so. Thus, necessity being the mother of invention, Betty being a Crocker, I figured if I were going to improve as a turkey hunter, I had better start studying. This meant more than just reading turkey books and listening to Lovett William's new turkey tapes. It meant trips to southeastern Ohio simply for the sake of getting into the woods, walking, sitting and watching turkeys. Needless to say, I made more trips to Vinton County for the purpose of scouting than I actually did for the purpose of hunting.

When the ODNR released turkeys in Logan County, north of Dayton, I traveled there on several occasions but did not see many turkeys. The most famous Logan County gobbler turned out to be the "Mad River Maniac," the one that attacked fly fishermen on the Mad River. The Daily News printed a photo of it, if I remember correctly, with several accounts of attacks and defense. My friend and artist, Phil Eddy, spent an enormous amount of time watching the turkeys in Wayne County, near Caesar Creek reservoir. To the best of my knowledge, he never ever shot one. He just watched, called and enjoyed their company.

I can almost say the same. I have spent thousands upon thousands of hours – do not tell my wife – in the woods watching turkeys. I have sat right under them as they flew up to roost and down the next day. To the effect that I have been anointed on several occasions with turkey poop. Which reminds me of one of my scouting expeditions to Pike County, Illinois.

It was in my early days in Illinois and I traveled often to the state wildlife area along the bluffs of the Illinois River. The area is named for some obscure state politician, who may or may not be in prison, and the name escapes me at the moment. Before the spring season opened, one March evening, Ian and I sat quietly on a hillside overlooking Blue Creek and waited for a flock of birds to arrive and roost. I had my video camera all charged up and loaded with a fresh tape. Around sunset, the birds appeared on the hilltop behind us. Silently, stealthfully, like Japanese soldiers in the old war movies, sneaking in for a silent attack on the Marines in their foxholes, the birds slipped up on us by surprise.

One by one, they launched into the trees around us. Before long, we had a humongous old gobbler roosting about 30 yards in front of us. I aimed the camera right at the bird and pushed the go-button. It stayed on the limb for several minutes and then, as gobblers are wont to do, it flew to another limb higher, and then another, higher, until it had circled farther up in the tree and almost out of sight. We watched the birds for close to 30 minutes and then we quietly sneaked away and back down the hill to the Jeep. We ended up with three old gobblers roosting above us. Farther south on the hillside, about 75 yards away, several hens inhabited the tree limbs.

If turkey season had been open, we would have returned the next morning, dark and early, and planted ourselves in between the gobblers and hens. This was the only tactic that I could think of that would have given us a chance to dispatch a bird. But, the season was still a month away and we were happy just to be alive, sit in woods and watch the marvelous birds go to roost. A 15-minute video of the event was icing on the cake. When Ian comes home from graduate school to visit, I offer to pop that particular video into the VCR for his entertainment pleasure but he offers some lame excuse and vacates the room. Maybe if I put one of those tapes in the refrigerator, he will leave my leftovers and beer alone, too.

In addition to actually watching turkeys, if you are fortunate, turkey scouting also includes looking for turkey sign – droppings, feathers, scratch, tracks – and deducing or reading it. One can become quite an expert at turkey sign with enough practice and a modicum of intelligence.

For example, you can figure out from the droppings whether you have hens, gobblers, young and old, in your neck of the woods. I once found a J-turd about the size of a candy cane in the far back field at Mr. Herring's farm here in Onslow County. I picked it up and examined it with the skill and acumen of Sherlock Holmes.

I therefore deduced that the bird was a gobbler of extraordinary proportions and age. It had been eating the succulent green tops of winter wheat. Since the turd was firm but not dry, some moisture left in it, light green and fibrous, I reasoned that the super gobbler had deposited this gift the evening before while dining on the wheat. Which was trampled with a meandering tunnel effect, stalk tops missing.

Lo and behold, now that I knew an extravagant gobbler was in the vicinity, I proceeded to locate this monster bird and discover that the double-bearded old giant roosted each evening along the creek bank and next to the wheat field. I proceeded to hunt this bird every morning I could. It proceeded to fly down and walk away every time it could.

From the turd size, lack of gobbles and stubborn deportment, I deduced the old gobbler to be a hermit and pronounced it "unhuntable". I refrained from giving it a name and proceeded to travel to Illinois and dispatch a dandy old gobbler there. If the super hermit shows up next season in the back field, I might consider messing with it a morning or two. But I ain't giving it a name.

Alas, turkey scratchings are very informative. You can deduce size of the flock, gender of the turkeys and direction of travel and time of travel from how the leaves and ground are torn up. A lot of scratch obviously means you have more than one turkey involved. Patchy scratch – a spot here and a spot there – can mean one bird or two or an old gobbler or two. Especially if the scratch spots are close to tree trunks. Gobblers tend to hit the tree trunk areas for nuts, seeds, grubs and insects. If the exposed earth in a scratch spot is still moist and no leaves or debris has fallen on it, the scratch is fairly fresh. If it is steamy, then the birds have been there recently.

You can predict the weather from turkey scratch, too. If it is wet, it is raining. If it is white, it is snowing. If it is dry, it is sunny. And so forth. An old Indian trick my Uncle "H" taught me.

Far be it for me to explain, expose and extrapolate all the fine and subtle qualities of turkey scratch and its divination. I will refer you to the voluminous tomes of turkey hunting books that cover this subject well. Suffice it to say, turkey scouting includes the delicate and graceful art of turkey scratch deduction.

Some of us simply have the gift.

Others, well, shall we say might need more field work and practice?

I took the photograph on page 40 while scouting for turkeys on a farm I hunt near home. That particular spring, three or four years ago, we had eight big gobblers and about two dozen hens visiting the soybean stubble field twice every day. First thing in the morning and later in the afternoon. The birds roosted in the cypress trees over a nearby beaver swamp. They flew down into a large grassy field and the hens immediately headed for the grocery store. The gobblers tagged along, strutting and gobbling.

I spent countless mornings and evenings watching and photographing these birds. Since I had done my homework and understood, as best as one can, the behavior and pattern of these birds, when hunting season finally arrived I was able to bump off one of the old toms one afternoon early in the season. It was a dominant gobbler and probably could have been sucked in with one of those new fandangled gobbler decoys. I did not use any decoys on that afternoon.

The reason why? The hens.

I discovered during my pre-season visits that when I placed a hen decoy in the field in hopes I could get the birds in close for a photograph, the hens tended to avoid the decoy like the plague. Therefore, one morning I invented the "reverse decoy" tactic just to see what would happen. I placed the hen decoy at the opposite end of the small 10-acre field and I hid in the brush at the other end.

Lo and behold, the hens arrived on schedule, strutting gobblers in tow, and proceeded to camp out right smack dab in front of me. They had absolutely no intention of visiting the decoy or going near it. I shot two rolls of film that morning under ideal light conditions. Early morning and late afternoon sunlight tends to accent the colors. The turkeys stayed for over an hour and were 30 to 40 yards away. From this preseason lesson, I learned to hunt this field without using a decoy. Especially since the gobblers stayed henned-up for most of the season.

This year I could not resist the temptation and invested in a Primos B-Mobile gobbler - named after "Bob" the stuffed gobbler. Let it be known that I bought it purely for scientific reasons. I did not use it very much during the recent spring season. The first time I used it I can truthfully report that the gobblers did not come running in like crazed Comanches in a war party hell-bent on taking scalps. Just the opposite reaction happened. A three-year old gobbler appeared in front of me late one morning while I hunted the back end of Black's Field at Rose Brook Farm in Missouri. It stood nervously observing the decoy and turned to walk away. Fortunately, I shot it before it escaped. So much for the TV commercial hype.

I will try the B-Mobile next spring during my pre-season scouting trips just to see what will happen and maybe, just maybe, shoot some great photos. Whatever the results, I should glean some good stories out of the experience.

I do not do much calling during my pre-season scouting trips. Especially on land and turkeys that I hunt. I don't want to educate them too early. I prefer to do my pre-season calling on other people's birds instead.

When I lived in the Midwest, I would call in birds on public land and take their pictures often. Since I could not get a permit to hunt these particular public land birds – I tried six years in a row but was not related to the Governor – I figured I would hone my calling skills on these birds. In addition, I probably did them a favor. I helped educate them and saved them from early elimination. A good preseason rule of thumb is do not call to your own birds lest you booger them up. Just watch them and keep out of sight.

I did mention the grocery store didn't I? An important key, probably the most important scouting key other than preseason gobbling, is locating the grocery store. As I had mentioned earlier, during my preseason scouting, I had located about two dozen hens visiting an old soybean field almost every day and twice a day. Thus, I knew from experience that the power of food was an important part of the formula for where the birds were going each day. Armed with this knowledge, I knew that, when the season began, trying to shoot a gobbler right off the beaver swamp roost would be a waste of time. My best bet was to be at the grocery store, the food source, and wait for the birds to arrive. I still had to call them in close enough for a shot. But, this beat the heck out of having a gobbler fly down, gobble like crazy and walk away.

If you can locate the grocery store, your chances of successfully dispatching a gobbler will rise significantly. I should add that the best grocery store is an old cornfield that has not been turned over. Turkeys just love to glean these fields and will visit them every day if left alone and unmolested.

I can't count the times, there are just so many, that I have encountered preseason turkeys, shot their pictures and watched their antics for hours on end. I have seen gobbler fights galore. Jake brawls and silly games. Hen fights. Hawk attacks. Coyote stalks. Gobblers doing the Turkey Lurkey and the Horizontal Mambo. You name it and I have probably seen it. Got the video, too.

One thing is for certain. I never get tired of watching wild turkeys. It has been said that the complete turkey hunter hunts both spring and fall turkeys. I would add that he or she also has the rare ability to find turkeys at any time of the year, photograph and videotape them AND watch those amateur videos, from start to finish, without a grimace or groan or bat of the eye.

Are you there yet? ↓↓

Chapter Three

"Boinky Boink"
Talking Turkey in Halifax

If the reader will be so kind as to revisit my first book, Chapter Twelve to be specific, you will rediscover that I am imminently qualified, accredited and otherwise deputized to pontificate, prevaricate and furthermore postulate on the various and sundry deviations, derivations and deputations of the wild turkey, its behavior, habitat and sexual deviations. I am a distinguished alumnus of that revered tower of ivory, the Pascagoula University of Taxidermy and Turkeyology. P.U.T.T. for short. Other significant alums include Doctor Bobby Dale, Ray Berryhill, Bob Gowen, Rudy Simione, Roy Rogers and George "Gabby" Hayes.

Forsooth. Since I occupy the lofty status of expert in epidemiological turkeyology, with a strong tendency to eat bugs and poop outdoors, I am in the unique position – sitting in front of my computer and typing on the keyboard – to elucidate the neophyte turkey hunter on the finer points of turkey vocabulary. Following in the footsteps of that beloved poultry pioneer, Lovett Williams, I wish to announce to the turkey world that I have discovered the 32nd turkey vocalization!

Lovett wrote in his wonderful masterpiece, *Wild Turkey Country*, Willow Creek Press, 1991, and I quote, "The wild turkey probably has more than 31 calls." Page 70. End of quote. In this chapter entitled, "The Turkey's Voice", Lovett highlighted about a dozen or so vocalizations, which most turkey hunters have heard at one time or another. He did not mention the "Boinky Boink." Leaving me with the conclusion that indeed I have discovered a new turkey sound. The "Boinky Boink".

An explanation is in order. And will take some time. So, put the book down, hit the head for a pit stop, then the frig for a cold one.

You're back? OK. The Boinky Boink call.

It happened last spring, while hunting in Halifax County with Bob Gowen, Bobby Dale and Ray Berryhill, that I discovered this new call.

Bob had left the farm to take Bobby and Ray to the airport in Raleigh. It was mid morning and, after saying goodbye to my buddies, I decided to trek down to the low ground along the Roanoke River and visit the cabbage patch, where Bobby had chased, unsuccessfully, a wily old longbeard for two days.

I was well familiar with the patch, having hunted it the previous spring and whereupon a rather fat and lengthy black snake had slithered noisily past my boots on its way to the creek behind me whilst I sat against an old oak tree and waited for turkeys to appear. When I arrived at the same tree, I carefully inspected the ground for snakes. Seeing none, I deemed it safe to sit and hunt. I then clipped a few green shoots and branches from brush nearby and stuck them in the ground around me for cover. Henry Davis would have approved.

My perch against the tree was quite comfortable and assured me I could sit there for several hours without pain or irritation. I settled in for the duration and softly called with my Quaker Boy Split Quad. My strategy was to call every 15 to 20 minutes and wait. I also decided not to use a decoy. The power of the patch (grocery store) and my seductive calling would be sufficient.

I did not have to wait long.

Fifteen minutes later, I noticed a dark form enter the cabbage patch from the opposite end, towards Bob's farm, about 60 yards away. It was a turkey, a hen, to be specific. I perked up, twisted around slightly, raised my gun barrel in its direction and yelped softly.

The hen cautiously stepped into the patch, inspected the field and proceeded to peck its way slowly towards me. I, on the other hand, thinking live decoy, began to watch the edge of the woods and point of entry for more turkeys. I figured a large mature gobbler, Bobby's Cabbage Patch longbeard, surely would soon appear, following the hen. This scenario has happened to me on more than one occasion in the past.

Lo and behold, another dark form materialized at the edge of the patch. I perked up and began to get excited. However, it was not the big boy. It was a young gobbler, head red and erect, eyes searching the open cabbage patch. Next, it proceeded to walk into the patch and follow the hen, pecking the ground as it moved forward. I softly yelped again.

And, another turkey appeared at the edge. And another one. And another one. All total, 14 turkeys in single file entered the cabbage patch and proceeded in my direction. But, they were all young gobblers. Not one longbeard amongst them. With one eye, I continued to watch the edge of the patch, still hoping a longbeard would arrive. With the other eye, I watched the flock of turkeys slowly working and feeding its way towards me.

It did not take long for them to arrive right smack dab in front of me. No more than 10 yards away. While they continued to peck and feed, oblivious to my presence, one bird would stand erect, eyes peeled for danger. I sat stone solid and watched the birds.

It did not take me long to figure, one, that a longbeard was probably not going to show and, two, that I was trapped. As long as 15 turkeys pecked and fed in front of me, I could not move unless I wanted to bust up the flock or shoot a Jake. Neither option appealed to me at the time.

I decided to bide my time, watch turkeys and hope that a longbeard might arrive and extricate me from my misery.

And misery is what it was. By this time, I had sat motionless for at least 30 minutes. My left leg was asleep, numb from knee to toes. My right hand was cramped around the trigger guard and the source of stabbing jolts of pain. To make matters worse, my bladder reminded me that it was way past time to eliminate the five cups of coffee I had consumed earlier that morning.

Forty-five minutes ticked away at a snail's pace.

The turkeys continued to occupy my corner of the cabbage patch and showed absolutely no inclination to depart or move away. My bladder and extremities had other ideas. But I hunkered down and remained still. I was not sure how long I could endure the pain but I hung in there.

Finally, the hen decided it was time to depart the patch. And it headed directly to me! It had the whole two-acre field from which to exit.

But, no. It was my corner and my tree that filled the bill. I stopped breathing.

Closer the hen approached until it passed by my paralyzed feet and legs. Then it stopped two feet away, looked right at me and softly called.

"Boinky boink."

Then it continued past me and right smack dab behind me and stood for the longest time, scratching in the leaves. I could have reached around and grabbed the darn turkey by the legs! Except for the fact that my arms were now numb and paralyzed, incapable of moving an inch. In fact, the only body parts that were not asleep, numb and stupefied were my eyes. And they were fast approaching the same set of circumstances.

Naturally, the young gobblers, all 14 of the sorry suckers, had to follow the hen. And, one by one, they walked right past me. Each stopped at my feet, stared me in the eyes, and softly proclaimed.

"Boinky boink."

"And boinky boink to you," I thought back. *"Now, for the love of God, get the hell out of my cabbage patch!"*

I reckon it took another five or ten minutes for the procession of poultry to depart. They lingered just behind me on the creek bank and scratched in the leaves. But, finally, thank the Lord, finally, they left.

And I flopped over on the ground. My body was asleep from head to toes. I waited for the blood to flow back to my arms and legs and for the awful pain that always follows. And, it did.

So there you have it straight from the horse's mouth. The "Boinky Boink" vocalization, all 15 times worth.

I have since heard this soft call on one more occasion whilst hunting turkeys with a local firefighter, Tee Tallman, at his family farm. Tee was sitting close to me, a couple of yards away, and he heard the calls, too.

We were sitting on a food plot, the 2007 NC spring season, early in the morning and waiting for birds to fly in. And, they did. They were all hens, no gobblers, and the first hen, walked by and ignored my soft calling.

The second hen, on the other hand, could not resist the sweet pitts and boinks and it walked right up to me and stood staring at my camouflaged profile. It stood there for several minutes – felt like an eternity – and softly *boinky boinked* back. Finally, it departed the field in the direction of loud gobbling down by the pond.

I am sure Tee will back me up on this veracity of this incident. Especially if he wants me to finish his wing bone call. I have his phone number and you can check with him. Just give me a call.

Lovett called the other day to clue me in on the meaning of "boinky boink". He is familiar with the call and tells me it means, loosely translated, "Way to go, dummy!" He says that turkeys use it to demonstrate their aggravation and disgust when one of their buddies does something stupid.

Figures. ↓↓

Tee Tallman's first longbeard.

Chapter Four

"Fall Fiasco"
Busted Glasses, Flu & Hawk Attack

Unbeknownst to me at the time, the 2001 fall turkey season would be my last fall turkey hunt at Rose Brook farm until the autumn of 2007. This particular fall hunt is memorable for two reasons. First, James Morris, the farm manager had spotted 15 adult gobblers using the pastures on the far east side of the farm. A part of the farm that was usually devoid of feathers, turds and tracks. And, he urged me to hunt them. And, I did. Although I was at first very skeptical.

Second, everything that could go wrong went wrong. From the very get-go.

I arrived at Rose Brook the night before opening day of fall turkey hunting. James showed me the best way to travel to the east side of the farm and the pasture where he had seen the 15 longbeards. Thus, the very next morning, I traveled over the dark, starlit pastures in my Jeep and arrived at the appropriate pasture in plenty of time to slip quietly down the fencerow and sit down in the tall grass, with my back to a stout fence post. No sooner had I sat down did I notice that the pasture and surrounding woods looked funny – fuzzy and weird. Strangely out of focus.

Now, if you turkey hunt long enough, you will notice that the woods and fields look very different in the dark than they do in the sunlight. But, this time they looked too different. Fuzzy and blurry. Suddenly, I realized that the problem was not the dark woods but me!

My glasses to be specific. My missing right lens to be exact! The darn thing had popped out while I was in the process of sitting down on the ground in the grass. Upon realizing the situation, a large knot expanded in my stomach and I panicked! My right eye was my shooting eye. How in the heck was I going to shoot a turkey without my right lens?

Well, I calmed myself down, pulled out my flashlight and began to look for the lost lens on the ground. With one good eye, the left. The right eye was useless in this situation. Luckily, for me, I found the lens quickly, as it was laying flat on the ground and reflecting the light. I picked it up and cleaned it off. So far, so good.

Next step. I needed to find out why the lens had popped out in the first place and fix the situation if I could. I examined my frames and discovered that the teeny, tiny microscopic screw, which holds the rim together, had disappeared, evaporated, gone missing. I glanced to the ground and realized quickly that I had a snowball's chance in hell to locate the miniscule screw. Therefore, I abandoned the search before it got started.

Instead, I thought duct tape!

Yep, duct tape that wonder of 20th century science, that cure for all things that break, burst, flap and flop, the tape that NASA invented to hold the heat tiles on the space shuttle when all else fails. And, best of all, I had a roll in the Jeep!

I dropped my gear and slipped quietly and quickly back to the Jeep, retracing my steps in the dark. Before long, I was performing rocket science magic in the light of my tailgate door. The tape slipped around the frames and, with some tearing and trimming, the right lens was re-attached to my glasses and I could see once again. Alleluia!

I headed back to the fencerow and sat down to wait for the dawn to break in the east over the Mississippi River, about five miles away. The soft breeze carried the sound of river tugs, the low rumble of their engines, pushing their barges and cargo up and down the river. For a few minutes, my thoughts left bad luck and turkeys and turned to Mark Twain, Tom Sawyer,

Huck Finn and the Old Man, the river. This old North Carolina boy was a long way from home and having a heck of a good time.

Now that I had repaired my glasses, I figured everything would turn out OK. When it got light enough, the predicted 15 gobblers would sashay out into the pasture. I would pick one out, squeeze the trigger and head home with Thanksgiving dinner. Nothing to it. I also figured I was due a quick hunt.

A quick fall Missouri hunt would allow me more time to hunt back home in Illinois and fill my tags. Then I would saddle up the Jeep and travel up to New York and chase birds with Art, Scott and the gang.

Yep, I was beginning to perk up and feel better about the morning and its prospects. When, all of a sudden, look out! A herd of husky Missouri whitetails busted out of the woods and dashed right smack dab into the middle of the 15-gobbler pasture. Whereupon, they stopped, looked in my direction and proceeded to stomp and snort so loud that the river men on the barges could hear the racket.

And so could the 15 gobblers, roosted on the side of the hill, next to the pasture.

When the snorts and stomps subsided, I could hear the clucks and cackles erupt from the hillside as 15 alarmed and disgusted gobblers flew down into the woods and went silent. So much for the idea of soft tree calling and coaxing the birds to fly down into the pasture. Moreover, if enough damage had not been done already, the deer completed the fiasco with a wild charge into the woods and straight into the flock of turkeys. I sat in silence and watched my chances for a quick fall hunt take a severe turn south and evaporate into the forest with the flash of the last whitetail's tail. Served me right for thinking such silly things in the first place.

Before long, silence returned to the forest and I called softly to the gobblers nearby. Nothing answered. Just more silence. So I relaxed a little, sat against the fence post in the fencerow and waited to see what would go wrong next. My quickie hunt for fall gobblers would take a little more time. No problem. I had all morning and all afternoon, if need be. I was just hoping to finish the hunt early.

Whilst I was napping just a bit, well hidden and motionless in the fencerow, I was awakened with a jolt when a tweety bird decided to flutter into the bushes and attempt to land on me. I do not recollect what kind of bird it was. It was small, noisy and brown. Probably a sparrow. Needless to say, it scared the Bejesus out of me and sent shock waves of adrenalin charging through my body. Likewise, I returned the favor and scared the heck out of it.

About this time, now that the sun was well up and casting dark, heavy shadows all around the pasture, I noticed a foreboding shadow gliding along the grass in front of me and heading for my lone hen decoy. I lifted my eyes to see a giant red tail hawk, swooping down from the sky, talons outstretched and heading directly for my plastic decoy. I watched in utter amazement as the hawk descended upon the decoy and, in one fell swoop, as they say, grabbed the thing and flew away! I immediately jumped up and starting yelling deleted expletives at the bird, as it gained altitude over the pasture.

I am not sure if my yelling made much difference or if the bird realized its prey was made of plastic. But, the hungry hawk dropped my decoy at treetop level and I watched it flutter ignobly to the ground.

Don't they say that bad things happen in threes? I had broken my glasses. Deer had busted me. A misguided hawk had stolen my decoy. All in all, opening day of Missouri fall season was off to a miserable start and I was beginning to consider going home before more bad things could happen – flat tire, dead battery, broken leg, heart attack. You name it, it could happen.

Being the patient persistent hunter that I am, I decided to push my luck and retrieve the decoy, plant it back in the ground and sit and wait some more. I walked across the field, picked up the decoy and returned to the scene of the crime. After staking it closer to me this time, just in case the hawk returned, I hunkered down in the fencerow and dozed off the sleep. I was feeling more tired and a little more achy than usual. I fell into a deep, fitful sleep.

When I awoke, I felt awful. I felt hot and feverish, my eyes burned, my muscles ached. Since I had exercised all summer, I knew I was in great physical shape for hunting season so my symptoms suggested that something else was wrong. Feeling poorly, I decided to cut my losses, cut the two-day hunt short and head home. I gathered up my stuff, walked back to the Jeep and drove back to the bunkhouse. James was out doing farm chores so I left him a note, explaining my early departure.

I began to feel worse not better as I drove back to Springfield, Illinois. I stopped in Pittsfield at McDonalds, bought a large soft drink and took some aspirin, which I carried in the glove box. I started to feel a little better when I finished the last leg of the trip and arrived home. My wife was surprised to see me but I told her I felt pretty bad – tired, achy, feverish. She retrieved the thermometer and proceeded to take my temperature. Whereupon she announced that I did have a fever and probably had the flu!

She was correct. I spent the next three days in bed, sick as a dog. I felt so rotten that I could care less about 15 gobblers or even 150 gobblers back at Rose Brook. All I wanted to do was sleep and maybe even die.

I did recover by the end of the week and felt well enough to return to Rose Brook and chase James's flock of gobblers. I spent most of that weekend, searching for the birds on the east side of the farm and beginning to doubt their existence. After a morning of frustration and no turkeys, I headed into Eolia for lunch. When I returned to the farm, I immediately spotted 15 black dots in the pasture leading up to what we now call "15 Gobbler Knob". I stopped the Jeep in the farm road, grabbed my binoculars and studied the situation.

Spread out in the pasture above me were 15 turkeys – all longbeards and identical. Same size beards. Same size turkeys. James had not exaggerated. There were 15 gobblers in this flock and on the east side of the farm, which usually does not hold many birds. I zipped over to the bunkhouse, retrieved my shotgun and drove up the hill road in hot pursuit of the turkeys. By now, the gobblers had casually disappeared uphill and into the woods. I proceeded to park the Jeep behind the big knob, hike up the back side and slip quietly into position at the top and looking down into the woods on the other side. I watched and waited.

Nothing.

Surely 15 gobblers, 300 pounds of wild turkey meat, would make a sound or become visible if I waited long enough. But, no sound or sign of turkeys came forth. Finally, I decided to move. I figured the birds had drifted east below the crest of the knob in the direction of the infamous pasture, where everything went wrong. I got up and followed the well-worn trail quickly and quietly to the east end of the ridge, carefully staying on top of the ridge and blocking sight of my movement.

When I reached the pasture, I examined it closely from above and saw no turkeys. I then figured the turkeys were still in the woods below, on the north face of the knob, and had not reached the pasture. I felt relieved that I did not have to mess with them in that cursed pasture. Instead, I slipped quietly down that face of the knob and stalked tree-to-tree back in the opposite direction. I would sneak up to a tree, stand behind it and coarse yelp softly. Before long, a gobbler returned my calls from ahead of me in the woods.

I slowly crept to another tree and repeated the process. The gobbler answered me again with three soft deep yelps. I watched and waited, hoping that the birds would change directions and head my way. They chose to continue their westerly course.

Again, I chose to close the distance and crept stealthily up to another tree, hid, called and watched. The gobbler answered me again. But, no turkeys arrived.

Finally, I saw the birds ahead of me, traveling casually around a bend in the knob and then disappear. One of the gobblers yelped, as if to tell me to come on. Which I did. With a new twist.

I had had enough of the tree hugging, calling and waiting for the gobblers to come to me. It was time to speed things up.

Since it was fall turkey season and I was completely alone on the north side of the knob, I knew it was safe to pull off my facemask, raise my shotgun to the assault position and deliberately charge into the turkeys. I would use the terrain, the bend to be specific, as my cover. The gobblers would not see me until it was too late.

Quickly and quietly, I moved forward at a rapid pace, slightly crouched over and charging like a soldier assaulting an enemy position. Gun raised and ready to fire. I also began to yelp softly, faking a straggling turkey trying to catch up with the flock. When I rounded the bend, lo and behold, you should have seen the look on those gobblers' faces! Were they surprised!

Spread out in front of me were 15 identical longbeards. I aimed at the closest one, fired and it dropped to the ground. The other birds panicked. Some flew off immediately. A couple ran away in the opposite direction. One or two flew straight up and landed in the trees above me. If, way back then, Missouri had allowed two birds to be taken on the same day, which it does now, I could have finished my limit right there and then. However, the new regulation was not in force, so I had to retrieve the dead gobbler – a dandy, I might add – and head back to the Jeep and drive 15 miles to Louisiana to check in the bird at Joe's Jug.

By the time I got back to the farm, it was too late to hunt the scattered flock of gobblers, which had probably begun to get back together anyway. I decided to wait until the next morning to continue the hunt. I had done enough damage for one day.

The next morning arrived early and I slipped into the scatter site, quietly in the dark. I found a good ambush spot, cut some branches and stuck them in the ground to fill in the holes in my natural blind. Then, I waited for the morning's first light and hopefully a few gobbler assembly yelps.

Just after first light, a couple of gobblers yelped from the woods west of me but nothing answered behind me from the east. I responded to the yelps with a few soft gobbler yelps of my own and waited. Before long, two adult gobblers appeared in the woods and cautiously advanced in my direction. They were definitely wary and took their time, slipping slowly and quietly through the forest. No turkeys or turkey sounds came from the woods behind me, which told me that the majority of the birds, which had flown in that direction, had probably gotten back together after I had left the evening before.

Alas, the two remaining longbeards decided to circle around my temporary blind and head in the direction where their buddies had flown the evening before. They had probably heard them re-assemble and decided to look for them since they could not see any birds in my location. Since I did not have a suitable gobbler decoy, I hunted without any decoy that morning. In retrospect, I do not think a decoy would have helped anyway. The birds walked around me and headed for where they thought the rest of the flock was.

After they departed, I decided to pack up my mess and head home. I would rather pursue these gobblers in the spring than mess with them anymore that fall. It was good to know that there were gobblers on the farm again, period. The previous spring was the first spring in 10 years that I hunted at Rose Brook, where I did not see or hear a mature gobbler. I had begun to think that I shot all the big toms on the farm. It was good to know that at least 14 gobblers would be around for the next spring season.

I have always been of the strong opinion that a complete turkey hunter is one who hunts successfully both in the fall and spring. I am surprised at how many "incomplete" turkey hunters pass up fall hunting and waste their time sitting in a tree stand and waiting for a deer not to show up. Or, worst still, they hunt waterfowl.

Many states permit fall turkey hunting and it is possible to hunt and shoot only gobblers, if you prefer that. I have taken a few hens in the fall season, all of which were mature birds and ended up on the dinner table at Thanksgiving and Christmas. But, fall turkey hunting is my favorite hunting.

Fall turkey hunting requires all the skills and expertise of hunting wild game. You must master the skills of finding and reading turkey sign. You must attain a very high level of woodsmanship and know your way around in the woods. You must match wits with the wild turkey, when it is in top form, at the top of its game. You will not find lovesick gobblers that crank up at the sound of a car door slamming shut. You will find wild turkeys that are super alert and focused on survival. To locate, track, call, sneak up on and otherwise hunt and shoot fall turkeys is the supreme test for the turkey hunter. My five-year-old grandson could probably call and shoot a gobbler in the spring, with a little help from me or his Dad. But, only a seasoned hunter, wise in the woods and experienced in the hunt, will consistently bring home turkeys for the holiday table.

I was watching a recent episode of Turkey Call TV the other day and the theme was fall turkey hunting. I was pleased to hear the narrator, Rob Keck, remark that to be a complete turkey hunter, one must hunt both fall and spring. Right on, Rob, and thanks!

For you "incomplete" turkey hunters out there, get out in the fall and hunt turkeys for a change. It might take you some time to get the hang of it but in the end, you will discover a whole new world to turkey hunting. If your state does not have a fall season yet, travel to one that does.

My friend, Bobby Dale, I am pleased to announce is now a complete turkey hunter. Bobby shot his first fall turkey this year. He was able to call in a whole flock and shoot a mature hen. Then he sent me the wing bones from the hen to make him a "replacement" wing bone call. Seeing how he lost the one-of-a-kind "Double Gobble" call, I had made him two years ago. Bobby said the fall hunt was too easy. He found a good spot, called in a flock right off the bat and shot his fall bird.

I reminded him that last fall; he had hunted for three days and did not dust a feather. He found fall turkeys but could not call them in or relocate them. Then, he spent the next two days looking for them and found nothing. I also reminded him that the easy hunt was pretty rare and to appreciate it for what it was. A gift from the turkey gods.

And a motivation to hunt fall turkeys again. ↓↓

Chapter Five

"Return to Rose Brook"
You CAN Go Home Again

Thomas Wolfe, a native son of Asheville, N.C., once wrote, "You can't go home again." In his case he was right on target. Since he had disparaged his hometown residents in his first book, *Look Homeward Angels*, he became *persona non gratis* back in Asheville rather quickly and for a long time. However, once he became more famous and had published more books, the local folks forgot, forgave and elevated Wolfe to hero status. But, his saying about going home is quoted often today. And, it is true to some extent. Time changes lots of people and places.

The last time I visited Asheville and my old neighborhood time had changed a few things.

For one, the old Beaver Lake golf course is now the Asheville Country Club golf course. And, second, my old neighborhood has turkeys! Wild turkeys, that is. We always seemed to have a few people turkeys living on Robin Hood Road back in my time. But, now they have real live wild turkeys, roaming the hills, woods, fairways and greens of the golf course and neighborhood,

Golf Course Turkeys, Asheville, North Carolina

    The last time I hunted Rose Brook farm in Clopton, Missouri was the spring turkey season 2002. At the time, I did not know it would be my last visit to the farm and that I would be moving back to my home state of North Carolina. Where, I might add, I did not repeat Wolfe's mistake. No discouraging words written or printed. During the 20-odd years I lived in the Midwest, I had been careful not to disparage, disrespect or otherwise burn bridges with my kin folk and friends back home. Forsooth, they were happy to see us when we returned semi-annually for visits, hunts and recreation. But, Spring 2002 would be my last turkey hunt at Rose Brook until the fall season of 2007. Five years later.

A lot can happen in five years. Wars started and not finished. Grandchildren born and going to school. Sons going off to war. And returning home safe and sound.

Five years is the average life span of a wild turkey, so I have read and heard. As for Rose Brook farm, the past five years have been pretty good and the turkeys have been fruitful and multiplied.

Its future, however, was in serious question when I left in August of 2002. Miss Rose's son was adamant about selling the place and moving his mother to Chicago. During the 2001 and 2002 turkey seasons, fall and spring, prospective buyers visited the farm and considered buying it. A two million dollar price tag may have slowed them down. But, a wealthy businessman from St. Louis eventually bought the place for a paltry $1.8 million to use as his family weekend retreat. He also purchased Mr. Black's 280 acres next door.

Best of all, he was smart enough to retain the services of James Morris as his farm manager and permit James to continue his cattle operation. Which generates a handsome income on the property. As for James, he moved out of the bunkhouse and into the large white tenant house near the breeding barn. The new house features a spare bedroom available for long-distance turkey hunters, such as me, to use whilst visiting and hunting turkeys.

The new owner also added a few useful improvements to the farm, clearing a nice trail around the Black property perimeter and carving a switchback ATV road up to the top of Hammer Ridge. The impact of these improvements is minimal and the total character of the farm remains unchanged. It is a rare and pleasant experience to return to a place after five years and discover that very little has changed.

On the downside, Bobby Dale and I discovered this past spring that five years of turkey hunting as not deterred or improved the Goober's skills or performance. The Goober showed up one morning in the Back Valley, late as usual, and, with poor calling as usual, tried to horn in on a gobbler that we had roosted and were working. The gobbler flew down, shut up and drifted away. Bobby and I did the same. I wish we had had the chance to take this bird quickly and out from under the Goober's nose. That would have been a heck of a story. Alas, it was not meant to be. At least, not this spring.

But, this chapter is about my return to Rose Brook in the fall of 2007 and a terrific fall hunt. I must admit I was as excited as a kid on Christmas morning to go back to Rose Brook and hunt fall turkeys once again. James's sister, Liz, filled me in on the events at the farm and helped me to get back in touch with her brother. A couple of phone calls sealed the deal and the next thing I knew I was stopping in St. Louis at the Bass Pro and buying a Missouri fall turkey license. A 40-minute drive up Highway 61 to Eolia, another 10 minutes to Clopton and I was back home at Rose Brook. I entered the back gate and drove across the shallow stream – no bridge yet – and up the gravel road to the white house.

    James was not there. He was out feeding cattle and working the farm, but he left me a note telling me to make myself at home and directions on settling in. I had not forgotten how to do that either. It did not take me long to unpack the Jeep, move in to the spare bedroom, change into my hunting clothes and hit the woods. When I had first arrived at the farm, I had stopped at the top of the hill to survey the pastures for turkeys. I spotted a flock of birds, 12 maybe 15, feeding in the lower pasture next to the breeding barn. They were in the back corner, as they always were, feeding on whatever cattle feed had spilled on the ground. Some things just do not change over time.

    I remember thinking that those turkeys were probably the third or fourth generation of birds that I had hunted at the farm. Yep, I had hunted their grandparents and even their great grandparents. I reckon the secret of the spilled cattle feed in the lower pasture had been passed down from generation to generation. That being the case, I also figured that the next thing this flock of birds would do is what their ancestors had done before – finish feeding, head back to the hole under the fence, scoot under and head up through the woods to the pasture known as Black's Field. They could chase bugs in the field then make their way back to Hammer Knob or Black's Valley and roost for the night.

Forsooth, I formulated my hunting strategy armed with the knowledge of previous fall hunts and turkey behavior. I bypassed the lower pasture and the birds in sight and headed for Black's Field. When I arrived at the field, again I noticed that nothing much had changed in five years. The bushes and trees had grown taller. I quickly found a good set-up spot on the edge of the field – a spot where I had shot several fall birds in the past – and settled in.

About an hour later and after a much-needed catnap, the turkeys from the lower pastured arrived as I had predicted. And from the direction I had expected. I had staked out a lone Bobble Head hen, as I had done in the past, and expected the flock to come to my calls. They did not.

The young birds in the flock spotted the decoy and got excited. They were about to come over and check out the new hen but the boss hen of the flock stop the advance with a loud cluck, almost an alarm putt. The cluck signaled that it did not recognize the intruder and suspected something fishy about the situation. The young birds fell in line and followed the older bird cautiously along the opposite edge of the field.

I answered the old hen with several soft yelps, purrs and sweet clucks, but it ignored me and led the flock off in the direction of the woods below Hammer Knob. As I watched the birds slowly depart, I figured it was just as well. I did not want to shoot a young bird, particularly so early in my fall turkey hunt. I was happy just to watch the birds, particularly the young ones and their goofy behavior.

Later that evening, I abandoned my set-up and headed for the woods below Hammer Knob. When I reached the woods, I sneaked along an old logging road, stopping often to listen for birds. As the sun began to dip below the western tree line, I began to hear birds calling to each other. Loud coarse yelps from older hens. Kee-kees from young birds. Next came wing beats. Sometimes from a single bird flying up to roost. Other times, wing beats from several birds flying up at the same time. As best I could figure, from the number of birds I heard fly up, there were several dozen birds roosting in the valley just below Hammer Knob. Armed with all the information I needed, I headed back to the farmhouse for supper and sleep.

That evening James returned from his chores and we had a wonderful visit. The past five years had been good to him and he caught me up on all that had transpired since I had moved back to North Carolina. I did the same for him. Before he went to bed, he also informed me, with a devilish smile, that since I had gone out "hunting" that afternoon, the score was Turkeys - 1 Preacher - 0. Nothing ever really changes. I was definitely back home at Rose Brook.

I woke up early the next morning and, after a cup of coffee and a Little Debbie cake, I left the house and headed back to the valley below Hammer Knob. The woods were still dark that hour before dawn but I knew my way down the trail with my eyes closed. I quickly and quietly slipped into an open area on a hillside facing the valley, found a good spot to set up and sat down. As the sunlight of the new day began to light the woods around me, the world woke up. Several deer slipped past without noticing me. Songbirds began to sing. From the woods north of me, back towards the breeding barn and lower pasture, a bunch of gobblers woke up and even gobbled to each other. A couple of hundred yards away, maybe closer, soft yelps and kee-kees announced that a large flock, maybe two, were occupying the valley and waking up, too.

Although it is unusual to call in an entire flock of turkeys in the fall, especially if the boss hen or hens have other destinations in mind, I usually give it my best shot and I did this time. I joined in with soft yelps and kee-kees. Before long, an old hen answered my calling with loud, almost demanding yelps, telling me to get moving and catch up with the flock. They were heading down into the valley and I was holding up the trip to the grocery store. I was tempted to get up and sneak along but I decided to sit still and play the obstinate young bird. A lesson my five-year-old grandson had taught me.

Well, the old hen and flock or flocks – there were lots more birds present than I had suspected – forgot about me and headed for breakfast. After they had drifted on down the valley, I got up and headed for the chunk of woods that held gobblers. Old habits die hard.

I crept down the hill, stopping and listening every few minutes, hoping to hear or see something up ahead where the gobblers had been roosting. Steadily I worked my way through the brush and woods until I reached the gobbler roost site. I saw and heard nothing. Just empty woods. The gobblers had flown down and disappeared into thin air. Which is nothing new. Turkeys do that all the time. From the sound of the coarse yelps and gobbles just 30 minutes earlier, I figured there were four maybe five old toms in total. Once they hit the ground, they, too, headed for breakfast and chances were that they avoided the large flock of young birds and old hens as best they could. More than likely, they had traveled west and away from the commotion.

Well, I spent the rest of that morning wandering the woods and checking out all of my old haunts and hunting spots where I had shot turkeys in the past. I sat for a couple of hours on the edge of the next valley over on Black's property, now part of Rose Brook, and called periodically down into the valley, thinking the small group of gobblers had headed there to feast on an abundance of acorns. In all probability, they were in the valley but they did not answer me.

I returned to the farmhouse around lunchtime and James and I headed to the Eolia Café to have lunch and visit with Miss Betty, James's new lady friend. Betty owns the café and the antique store next door. While we devoured the special of the day, Betty visited with us and proved to be very sweet, charming and entertaining. After lunch, we headed back to the farm. James back to work. I headed for the bedroom and a short nap.

Later that afternoon I headed for the lower pasture and set up in my old clump of cedar trees. I arrived in plenty of time in case the flock that was feeding there the day before returned this day. To make a long story short, the flock did not show up. Which puzzled me since I had not boogered them the day before. However, the woods were full of large, succulent acorns and the fields were crawling with grasshoppers and crickets. Rose Brook had plenty of groceries for hungry turkeys almost everywhere. I guess the menu for that afternoon did not include spilled cattle feed.

Before sunset, I left the cedar trees and climbed, along the fencerow, up the hill opposite the valley below Hammer Knob. When I reached the top, I sat down on a stump, rested and listened for turkey sounds. As I watched the sun start to touch the western tree line in the distance, I began to hear turkeys flying up to roost. Again, the birds had selected the same spot in the valley as they had the previous evening. I tried to count the number of birds but it was hard to tell just how many had flown up. Suffice it to say, it was a large flock or two.

I retreated back down the hill and headed for another evening with James at the farmhouse. And, as usual, James informed me, with a twinkle in his eye and a chuckle, that the score was now Turkeys – 2 Preacher – 0.

He added, "You are so far behind now, you will never catch up."

I went to bed early and fell fast asleep. My last thought, I think, was the more I try to catch up, the behinder I get. Did James allow me to hunt Rose Brook turkeys simply because he enjoyed keeping score? Pictures of Sisyphus pushing the rock up the hill floated in my dreams.

I was up early the next morning and heading back to the valley below Hammer Knob. I slipped silently into the woods and sneaked back to the same spot I had used the day before. As the morning broke, the events from the day before began to replay. The same deer passed by and ignored me. The songbirds sang and the gobblers gobbled down by the breeding barn woods. But, this time, the large flock of young birds and hens were much closer. Once again, I joined them in their tree calling. However, on this morning, events turned differently.

Two flocks were roosted in the surrounding trees. One group flew down, assembled and headed up the hill along the side of Hammer Knob. The other flock, however, decided to visit me. Before long, I spotted an adult hen, leading a variety of young hens and young gobblers in a single file, heading straight for me. I adjusted my position to face the oncoming line, shouldered my shotgun and rested the fore end on my knee. Before long the old hen appeared at the end of my muzzle and stopped. It stood erect and its eyes took a direct bead on me - the funny looking bush that was up against an old oak tree.

At the same time, I fixed the red dot on my sight to the turkey's neck and squeezed the trigger.

The shot shattered the early morning stillness and the old hen flopped over dead. The remaining birds went berserk. Some ran off. Others flew away. A couple just stood there, stupefied. Although the state permits you to shoot two birds in the fall on the same day, I decided that one was enough for the moment. After I retrieved the dead hen, a large adult, I sat and waited for the remaining birds to regroup. About 20 minutes later, I could hear the young birds kee-keeing and yelping to each other. Birds from the other flock on the hillside above me began to answer the scattered birds below. It did not take long for the lost birds to find a new home. Up the hill with real turkeys.

I headed back to the farmhouse. The score was now Turkeys – 2 Preacher – 1. James was right. Since I could only harvest two birds legally, I might catch up but I could not win. The score did not matter. I had dispatched another fall turkey at Rose Brook after a five-year hiatus. This bird was bound for the freezer and would lead a new life (in death) back in North Carolina as a hen decoy for Tee Tallman, my turkey-hunting apprentice.

After another lunch at the Eolia Café and visit with Betty, I caught a quick nap back at the farmhouse. I spent the afternoon trying to locate the group of gobblers that had so far eluded me. I ended the hunt, waiting for the birds to return to their roost site. They did not. Obviously, they had moved to greener pastures and I did not have a clue.

On the other hand, I was anxiously awaiting Doc Lucky's arrival from Springfield, Illinois, about an hour and a half drive from Rose Brook. The circle would be complete once Doc arrived and we headed back into the woods to chase fall turkeys together. If memory serves me, I do believe Doc shot his first turkeys, in the fall, and with me at Rose Brook. The year, however, slips my mind. We kept in touch by cell phone that afternoon.

Doc arrived that evening and we proceeded to visit with James and eat supper.

James updated Doc on the score and informed him that there was no way I could win now, not even with Doc Lucky onboard and helping out. In fact, Doc's presence would double the numbers. We chuckled at James's math and offered weak excuses. The circle was complete. Doc was back at Rose Brook. All was quiet on the Western Front. Life was good.

We were up early the next morning and after a quick bite to eat, we headed to the woods. Since I could not locate the mystery gobblers, I figured our best bet was to start in Black's Valley, for old times sake, where I thought the gobblers had gone and where Doc and I had killed our first fall turkeys at Rose Brook. I parked the Jeep at Black's Field and we hiked west. Soon, we slipped into the woods and settled in to the spot where we had killed those first birds many years ago. The spot had not changed.

A wide and open hillside looked down into a valley that ran north and south. I had killed my last spring turkey, with the help of Doc's finishing shot, in this valley five years earlier. The valley always held fall turkeys – gobblers and flocks of young birds and hens.

As the sun slowly appeared in the east, behind us, we watched the valley become more visible. I called a few soft yelps and kee-kees but no birds responded. After sunrise, we heard loud footsteps in the dry leaves, coming from the valley below and heading in our direction. Soon, we spotted three deer traveling up the hill and towards us. We hunkered down and watched closely as a yearling, a doe and a hefty eight-point buck arrived. Ignoring us, the deer lingered for a long time, munching on acorns and acting frisky. If we had been bow hunting instead of turkey hunting, the eight-pointer would have been traveling back to Illinois with Doc Lucky. The buck presented several opportunities for broadside shots at 30 yards or less.

Had we been bow hunting for deer, we would have seen none and a flock of 100 turkeys would have closed in on us instead. It never fails.

We enjoyed the deer show and they finally headed up the hill and towards Hammer Knob. It was time to leave and seek turkeys elsewhere. We decided to take a short hike east and return to the scene of the previous morning's crime. I did not expect any birds to have roosted there due to the events of the previous morning. However, I did expect them to be close by. They were.

It was now midmorning when we arrived at the hillside where I had shot the old hen the day before. I settled in and hid in the limbs of an old blown down tree, while Doc sat down slightly uphill and to my left against a large oak tree. After we got comfortable, I began to call out a series of lost yelps and kee-kees. Since I was thirsty and a tad hungry, I took a break from calling and reached into my vest for my water bottle and snacks.

While I was munching away and enjoying the beautiful, cool autumn morning, I heard Doc calling from behind. Soft coarse yelps and I thought to myself, "*Boy, Doc has really learned to call well since I have been gone.*" I settled in to enjoy my snack and drink. Doc could do the calling while I did the snacking. Another series of soft coarse yelps wafted through the woods but something was different this time. The yelps were closer and very realistic!

I dropped my snacks, grabbed my shotgun and slowly turned to look in Doc's direction. Lo and behold, a large hen turkey stood behind me and surveyed the hillside below. No wonder Doc's calling sounded so good. The calls came from a real turkey! About 25 yards uphill.

I slowly adjusted my position and aimed my shotgun at the hen nearby. It was then that I realized that I did not have a shot. Doc Lucky was in the line of fire! Just beyond the hen, about 30 yards of so. I quickly did the mental math. Doc Lucky versus dead turkey. If I shot the turkey and hit Doc, too, his wife would never forgive me. Not to mention the lawsuit. Therefore, I waited for the hen to move.

Kablaam! A shot roared above me from Doc's shotgun.

The hen turkey, at which I was aiming, jumped up and flew away. Another bird, on the other side of Doc, ran off into the woods. Moreover, another one jumped up and flew out and over me, heading for parts unknown. Unbeknownst to me, I had called in a small flock of birds. And, as far as I could tell, Doc had missed the hen.

When the dust had settled, I cautiously whistled to Doc and then stood up slowly.

"Hey, did you shoot and miss that hen?" I shouted.

"What hen?" answered Doc.

"The hen that was behind me and calling," I shouted back.

"What hen? I thought that was you calling," said Doc.

"No, wasn't me. I was eating a snack and thought YOU were calling. If you didn't see the hen, then what the heck did you shoot?"

"I shot the big Jake that walked out right in front of me," said Jeff, now up and walking down to me. He raised his arm and pointed down the hill to where a turkey lay lifeless.

"I'll be darn. All I saw was that one hen above me and I could not shoot because you were behind it and in the line of fire. I figured Theresa would be pissed if you did not come home."

"You called in a small flock of birds, maybe six or seven or more," said Doc. "They were all around me, behind me, beside me. Then the Jake walked by and when it got about 20 yards out, I let the pellets fly."

"I see you did and congratulations on a good job. Let's see. The score is Turkeys – 2 and Team – 2."

We inspected the young Jake and traveled back to the farmhouse. James was waiting for us and checked Doc's bird out before announcing the results of the morning hunt.

"Gentlemen. The score is Turkeys – 4 and Hunters – 2. Since you hunted together, that makes you a team. I had to double the number. You fellows need to do a better job than that."

We did not argue. Knew better.

That afternoon we headed to Illinois for opening day of fall season the next day. Our old friend, Joe Lindley would join us at the Cass County farm and I would end up calling in three big Lincoln Land gobblers, gobbling their heads off and in full strut. Twice.

But, that is another story.

For another day. ↓↓

The Team: Doc Lucky and the Preacher

Chapter Six

"Creating Monsters"
Wasting Away in Margarita Ville

Jimmy Buffet, in that classic tune, *Margarita Ville*, croons that he has a brand new tattoo, a real beauty, a Mexican cutie, and how it got there he hasn't a clue. Some people say there's a woman to blame, but he thinks it could be his own fault.

I'm not quite sure that tattoos and monsters are related. But there is a sliver of relevance somewhere in this introduction. I don't have a tattoo. Moreover, ancient scarification rituals don't interest me. I do know, however, a fellow in New York, who has a turkey tattoo on his arm. Furthermore, I don't have a clue as to why we create monsters, but we inevitably do and I suspect it is our own darn fault.

Case in point. I got a pretty good picture of my monster-creating ability, way back, when I took my wife fishing for the first time. We went surf fishing on the beach at Emerald Isle in our new Jeep CJ7. To make a long and painful story short, she caught all the fish – speckled trout – and I got skunked. I did all the work. Rigged the rods; baited the hooks; showed her how and where to cast; the whole nine yards. She caught all the fish. I caught none.

One could argue that I spent a lot of time tending to her needs and less time fishing myself. But, truth be known, I am the poster boy for the old saw, "No good deed goes unpunished." It was my own darn fault.

That was the last time I invited her to go fishing with me and so far, after 36 years, she has not asked to go again. Nor have I brought up the subject. I reckon you could say I had created a fish-catching monster. But, I had the good sense to dine on humble pie and move on. As she would say, "Go to Lowe's; buy some lumber; build a bridge and get over it."

Moving on. The second monster, which I have created and about whom you have read, is my oldest son, the die-hard waterfowler. He loves to hunt everything. You name it, he hunts it. Wild turkeys are definitely on the list. However, waterfowl – ducks and geese – reside at the top at the present moment. I am sure as he grows older and wiser – short of breath, long of tooth – he will scratch out waterfowl and insert wild turkeys in the Number One spot. For the time being and as long as he is able, he will chase ducks.

There is no one to blame for his condition but myself. It is my fault. I, too, had the same zeal in my youthfulness and made the mistake of taking him duck hunting at the ripe young age of 10. Since then, he has yet to slow down. His son shows the same tendency and will wander down that path of pleasant misery unless I intercede, intervene and otherwise interfere.

My plan is simple. Get there firstest with the mostest. I will take my grandson turkey hunting way before his mother will allow his father to take him duck hunting. I will show him the wonderful beauty and WARMTH of spring mornings in the woods. We will hunt in my big blind, where he can MOVE all he wants. I will encourage him to whack away at the box call I gave him last year. Most of all, he will come home with a gobbler as big as he is. No excuses, no ice or mud. No Jack Frost!

Now, if he does not place turkey hunting above waterfowl, he is obviously not really related to me. A DNA test would be in order.

Another of my monsters, again you have read about him, is my second son, the fly fisherman. Same painful story, so here is the short version. I took him fly fishing for the first time when he was five or six in the Davidson River, where I learned to fly fish when I was about 10 or so. He was a natural at fly-casting and still is. When I mention turkey hunting, he counters with fly-fishing. End of story. There is no hope for this son. But I will keep trying. We plan a post Master's Degree turkey hunt in Kansas this spring. At some point between now and then, I am sure he will suggest a fishing trip instead.

(The aforementioned Kansas hunt did not pan out as planned. The oldest son had to travel to Joint Command in Suffolk for a planning conference. As predicted, the youngest son suggested a two-day trip to Montauk and the Current River to fly-fish and I relented. In spite of bad weather, we caught fish and ate rainbow trout for dinner.)

I am sure I have created many monsters over the years while introducing friends to the fine and pleasant art of turkey hunting. Only one resisted the charm, the magnetic pull, the cosmological rush of wild turkeys. Uncle Doug, my dearly departed brother-in-law. On the other hand, Doc Lucky went with me to Rose Brook one fall, a long, long time ago, shot his first turkey and the rest is history. The man is a turkey-hunting monster of the first magnitude. Thanks to me.

I reckon it is only human to create a few monsters along the road of life. When it comes to wild turkeys, we create them all the time. I'm talking about the turkeys we hunt that whip our butts. We take it personally. We give those gobblers names. And we hunt them day after day, year after year. Pretty soon, it becomes obvious that these birds quickly learn our tricks, turn the tables on us and beat us every time. The Hammer was one of those birds. Perhaps he was the greatest monster that I have ever created.

The Hammer appropriately resided on Hammer Knob at Rose Brook Farm in Clopton, Missouri. He was the boss gobbler of the farm and demonstrated his dominance every chance he got. Not only did he whip the butt of every bird unlucky enough to run into him, but he whipped every hunter, too. Doc Lucky. Mark Faull. William Hurt. Bill Crum. John Harris. Uncle Doug. And me. Just to name a few.

The Hammer earned his name from his obnoxious habit of flying to roost every night – in the same tree on the east side of the knob, almost at the top – and "hammering away" like a pileated woodpecker. You could set your watch by his fly up time. Sunset. Just as soon as the sun dipped below the tree line that split Rose Brook from Mr. Black's farm, the Hammer would fly up in his tree and gobble 50 times.

He gobbled so much and with such cocky predictability that we got lazy and simply roosted him by walking out the front door of the bunk house, standing in the front yard and waiting for him to rattle away at sunset. He never failed to show up and perform. We should have named him "Old Faithful" instead of the Hammer.

I first encountered this despicable bird while hunting with Doc Lucky on the ridge that led to Hammer Knob. We had roosted another bird, closer to us than the Hammer, on the ridge the previous evening and decided to hunt it the next morning. Early the next morning, we drove up the hill road that splits the farm in two, parked in the pasture at the top and hiked quickly and quietly up the backside of Hammer Knob. We used an old deer trail that gently angled up the ridge instead of hiking straight up the face of the north precipice and into a heart attack. Early on, we had discovered that we had better luck working those Missouri toms if we could get above them or at their level. We rarely could get them to come down to us, at least first thing in the morning.

    We reached the top of the ridge with time to spare and sneaked silently eastward along the trail at the top. When we reached the spot where the gobbler was roosting, we split up a little bit and sat down. Doc sat down next to the trail to cover the bird if it went west. I sat down about 30 yards up the trail, next to the property fence, in case the bird went east. If it decided to travel south, it would have to walk right between us. We figured we had all the avenues covered.

    As the new light of day gradually invaded the hardwoods around us, our gobbler announced its presence with a loud and lusty gobble. It was roosted about 75 yards at the most from us and we were in excellent set-up spots. We watched, waited and listened. The bird continued to gobble every few minutes or so and when the time came, I answered with a couple of soft tree yelps on my little Jet slate call, "Sweetness". The woods became quiet and I could picture the bird, cocking its head to one side, and zeroing in on my position.

A minute or two later, the bird gobbled again and it was evident that the tom was now facing me and gobbling with a purpose. I did not return the favor and kept quiet.

After the third and almost desperate gobble, I responded with some soft, perky, sexy yelps that intimated a tad of interest on my part. The tom double gobbled back, cutting off my last yelp. At this point, I realized that the web was spun and I pocketed my slate and striker. The bird was focused, frenzied and frantic. It needed no more persuasion. I continued to listen to the surrounding sounds of the woods in hope that no hens were present to mess up the deal. The woods remained void of hen chatter. Just a few tweety birds chirped merrily away from the branches nearby.

It did not take long for wing beats slashing against the branches and leaves to signal that the tom was coming down and heading right for us. I shouldered my shotgun, pointed it in the direction of the commotion and waited. I watched Doc do the same on my left.

The bird pitched down just below us and temporarily out of sight. The crest of the ridge blocked our view. We heard a loud thump and then an explosive gobble shook the ground beneath us. We both knew that within seconds a fiery red head would periscope up over the ridge. It was simply a matter of who got the shot, who was closest to the bird.

The dry leaves crunched as the gobbler climbed the knob and closed in. The tension mounted. My grip tightened on my gun. I held my breath.

"GOBBBBLE! GOBBBBLE!"

What the heck? Another bird had approached from the west and was right behind Doc. The Hammer had arrived!

Forsooth, the old tom had heard the commotion down the trail from his roost and decided to nip the shenanigans in the bud, once and for all. While we were mesmerized with the impending appearance of the first tom, the Hammer swooped down from his roost tree, glided a couple hundred yards down the ridge trail and landed right smack dab in the middle of things. Only one gobbler was king of the hill and it was the Hammer.

"GOBBBBLE! GOBBBBLE!" The Hammer challenged the interloper. Preferring discretion to valor, the other tom remained silent. Loud, crunchy footsteps in the dry leaves signaled its retreat down the hill.

The easy bird was gone in a flash, taking with it our chances of shooting a gobbler that morning. I slowly shifted my position to the left and now faced west and the ridge trail. I scrutinized the woods, looking for the least bit of motion. Nothing moved.

I carefully slipped into position the Quaker Boy Split Quad, which had been nestled between my gum and cheek like a packet of snuff, and sent forth excited cuts followed by soft yelps. Nothing answered. I watched and waited.

A few minutes later, the Hammer gobbled again but he was farther away and heading back to his part of the knob. His job was done. The challenger was banished. He did not seem to care about the prize. Doc Lucky and me.

I called again. Excited. Forlorn. Begging. Pleading. The Hammer finally gobbled back, almost a courtesy gobble at this point. He was almost home and not much interested. I got up and quickly walked over to Doc.

"Well, did you see him?" I asked.

"Nope. I did not. I was afraid to move. He was so close that the first gobble blew my hat off and the second one scorched my moustache!" Doc exclaimed.

"Did you get a look at the first tom?" I continued, trying to size up the situation and develop a game plan.

"Almost. Another second and I think the end of my gun barrel would have covered its head," replied Doc, confidently.

"Dang it." I said. "Dang it. Dang it. Dang it. We had that easy bird wrapped up, leg tagged and toted down the hill. Then, the Hammer had to show up and shut us down. It ain't fair."

"What you think now? You got a plan?" Doc inquired with thoughts of pursuing the Hammer.

"I guess we will have to sneak down the ridge trail and try to shake Hammer's tree. I don't think we have a snowball's chance, but we can try."

Forsooth, try we did and even with the luckiest turkey hunter alive, Jeff "Doc Lucky" Bierman, the Hammer answered not. The Hammer responded not. He ignored us and left us butt-whipped and foolish.

We retreated down the knob and back to the bunkhouse for the loser's meal – a cold breakfast of crow and a generous slice of humble pie. Turkeys – 2 and hunters – 0.

As best as I can recall, and it has been several years ago and painful memories are pushed to the back of one's mind, that was my first close encounter with the Hammer. From that point on, the relationship became personal and I spent way too many mornings hunting that old bird and trying to kill it. And so did Doc.

We decided to go after the Hammer the very next morning. That evening we proceeded to the front yard and listened to him hammer away at sunset on Hammer Knob. We could almost see him in his roost tree, high on the knob and backlit with fading orange sunlight. His obnoxious gobbling seemed to proclaim his superiority, while rubbing salt in our wounds.

We woke up early the next morning, grabbed a bite to eat and gulped some coffee fast, then headed up the dirt road that split the farm in two and ended at the pasture below Hammer Knob. In silence, we slipped up the back trail without making a sound. When we arrived at the top of the ridge, we headed west on the ridge trail and sneaked into position about 100 yards or less from the Hammer's roost tree. We found a dead tree, collapsed on the ground, crawled into its limbs and branches and hid. The tree offered an excellent natural blind and the Hammer should not notice us, hidden within it.

And, as Henry Davis had warned in his book, *The American Wild Turkey*, 1949, there is such a thing as too good a blind. Davis was an ardent apostle of building natural blinds and calling in wild turkeys. He also warned that the hunter should be careful not to "over build" the blind so as to eliminate any chance of moving his shotgun or shooting.

Well, our blind was simply too good. As soon as we hunkered down between the limbs and branches of the dead tree, it was evident that we were surrounded by dead tree brush and new growth and could not see more than 10 feet in any direction. We were stymied and before I could devise a tactical withdrawal to more open ground, the Hammer decided to fly down, land right in front of us and gobble his head off.

He was so close that the ground shook with each roaring gobble. The tom was so close you could actually feel the air move when he gobbled. Yet, we could not see a thing. Not a feather or tailfan. No red or white head poking up through the brush. On the other hand, we could almost hear the darn turkey breathing. He was that close. All we could do was sit tight, guns poised for action and pointed in the direction of the old bird, and wait.

Before long, we heard the Hammer crunching the dry leaves in front of us, as he began to walk up to us and then veer to the left, to Doc Lucky's side of the dead tree, and go around. The old rascal walked right by Doc Lucky and we did not see a thing.

In hindsight, Doc probably could have jumped up and taken a quick shot at the bird because the bird had no clue we were hunters. More than likely, Doc would have had a second or two to get the shot off. I have seen him in action and he could have pulled it off. However, at that time we were more conservative in our hunting methods and figured the old tom would give us at least a quick peak and an opening through which to shoot.

The next gobble revealed that the Hammer had indeed walked right past Doc and was now anchored behind us, maybe 30 yards away. I called to him on my Split Quad and he answered. Every time. But, the wise old gobbler would not budge from his spot. Nor did he give us a visible target to shoot.

The next time he gobbled, he was obviously on the move and heading west towards the next knob, Black's Knob. Once I realized this, I whispered to Doc to slip out of the "blind" and put a flanking maneuver on the bird. I would sit tight and continue to call. That way Doc could maintain a perspective on things. He could hear me calling and the Hammer responding as it slowly traveled west. All he had to do was get around the old bird, find a good spot to set up and wait for the bird to arrive. I have come to call this tactic, flanking and reverse calling.

If it is safe to do so, one hunter carefully flanks the hung-up gobbler and gets ahead of it once the direction of travel is discovered. The other hunter sits tight and gets the bird to gobble periodically. In most cases, the gobbler probably has a hen or two with it and it is the hens that lead the bird away. In the case of the Hammer, he was alone, as far as we could tell, and had learned through the years that either the hen he heard would come to him or he would walk away. I had probably taught the Hammer that not every hen he heard was a real turkey hen.

The flanking hunter, also, does not call. He simply locates a good ambush position, takes cover and waits for events to unfold. He may need to call a little and softly, once the gobbler is close and needs a little coaxing. He is imitating a hen that has heard all the gobbling and has arrived to see what is going on.

Back to the Hammer. After sufficient time, Doc had gained the advantage on the Hammer and placed himself ahead of the traveling tom. I remained in the dead tree and continued to call every few minutes with different series of excited cutts and yelps. The Hammer continued to gobble back two or three times as he slowly traveled away. As far as I could figure, enough time had passed. Doc should have been able to hear everything, size up the situation and now be in position to whack this cranky old tom as soon as he could see him. I began to anticipate a gunshot and an end to this foolishness.

However, I heard no gunshot and the Hammer continue to travel west, gobbling every now and then. He finally reached a point where he was too far away and my calling was futile. Since Doc was on the prowl, somewhere out there, I decided to sit down on a stump, light my pipe and enjoy the cool spring morning. I had officially withdrawn from contest and was now a mere spectator.

The minutes ticked away and the gobbles grew sparser and fainter. No gunshots rang out either. From the sound of things, the contest must have concluded with the Hammer escaping Doc's mighty Mojo. The old gobbler did not know how lucky he had been. Eventually, Doc appeared in the woods, walking slowly, head hung low and shotgun dragging the ground. I have never seen a more vivid picture of a dejected hunter.

"What the blue blazes happened?" I inquired of the depressed turkey hunter.

"I screwed up," answered Doc. "The Hammer got away."

"Did you see him?" I asked.

"Yep, face to face. As close as I am to you. The plan worked perfectly. I got way ahead of him and waited. I could hear you calling and the Hammer coming my way."

"And?"

"When he got close, everything got quiet. I waited and waited. Nothing. Then I poked my head out from around a tree and there he was, ten feet away! Before I could get my gun on him, he took off like a rocket and flew down into Black's Valley."

"Unbelievable," I muttered and reached into my turkey vest to pull out a white flag of surrender.

The Hammer escaped all of our tricks and lived a long life on Hammer Knob. We hunted that bird many more mornings, too many mornings, only to have more of the same results. Close but no cigars. When I hunted alone, I spent the rest of that season and several more seasons, hunting only that bird and did not get a shot. Not even close. The Hammer was, without a doubt, the toughest old bird I have ever hunted.

The last time I saw the Hammer was when Uncle Doug accompanied me to Rose Brook and, on the only morning it did not rain, we bumped into him by accident – I had learned by then to give him a wide berth – and watched him fly away and down into the valley to disappear into history.

"Holy Cow!" exclaimed Doug. "That was a huge gobbler. Why aren't we hunting it?"

"Because," said I matter-of-factly, "that was the Hammer and he will beat your six foot eight inch butt to a pulp. We best leave him alone. Trust me." And, we did.

These are but two of the many and futile clashes over a period of five spring and fall turkey seasons with the infamous Hammer. I doubt that I will exposit, extrapolate and otherwise elucidate on any more those hunts. The pain is too deep and, following my wife's advice, I have gone to Lowe's, bought the lumber, built the bridge and got over it.

I will add this concluding anecdote, howsumever. I killed an old tom in the Holly Shelter Swamp, three years ago. The Swamp Daddy. It took me almost nine hours to kill this bird. However, it behaved much the same as the Hammer and, having learned many valuable lessons from the old Hammer, I was able to win this contest. Fortunately, we can hunt all day in North Carolina and I was able to kill this bird in the afternoon. The reader will find that story in Chapter Two of my first book, *Bend Over, Shake A Tailfeather!*. If I could have hunted all day in Missouri, instead of having to quit at 1 p.m., I might have beat the Hammer at his own game.

We will never know, will we? ↓↓

Chapter Seven

"Turkey Deja Vu"
Your next stop - the Turkey Zone

Déjà vu, says Webster, is something overly familiar. In French, déjà vu literally means "already seen." Yogi Berra reminded us, "It was déjà vu all over again." In turkey hunting, it means you are about to enter - close your eyes and imagine Rod Serling is narrating this – a special place.

"There is a fifth dimension beyond that which is known to man. It is a dimension as vast as space and as timeless as infinity. It is the middle ground between light and shadow, between science and superstition, and it lies between the pit of man's fears and the summit of his knowledge. This is the dimension of imagination."

You are traveling through this dimension, a dimension not only of sight and sound but of mind. That's the signpost up ahead – your next stop, the Turkey Zone.

Picture, if you will, a mild-mannered man in his mid-30s. Average height. Average weight. He is in excellent physical health and is able to climb the mountains of southeastern Ohio with relative ease. He is a turkey hunter and has traveled from Dayton to Vinton County for opening day of spring turkey season. The time and date aren't relevant.

The man sleeps in the back of his van, awaiting another chance at destiny.

An annoying mosquito-like buzz woke him up. His travel clock's reliable alarm. In the distance a lonesome freight train rumbled its way north, horn wailing every minute or so. The man sat up in the back of his van, rubbing his eyes, his body stiff from sleeping on the hard floor.

He had been dreaming about turkeys again. He leaned against the front seat and tried to remember the dream. He couldn't quite picture it. He groped for his glasses and flashlight. It was 5 a.m. Opening day of spring turkey season. His mind turned to more important things – revenge.

It was hard to believe that a year earlier he had finished the season by leaving a wise old tom in the woods nearby. He had named it "The Heartbreaker". For five mornings in a row, they had matched wits. Through two hellacious thunderstorms complete with torrential downpours, he had waited the tom out. But no matter what the hunter did, the old bird made a fool of him. It used every trick it knew and invented a few new ones to escape his shotgun. The hunter used every trick he knew to get that bird. In the end, the situation got personal.

But, that was a year ago. This morning was the beginning of a new season, a second chance.

The man slipped out of his toasty sleeping bag and dressed without thinking. His mind was elsewhere; up in the hollow where the big tom roosted in its favorite sycamore tree – a roost preference the hunter had discovered AFTER the last season had ended.

That's right. The man had hunted the old bird after the season was over – not with a gun, but with a camera. The hunter had wanted to find out everything he could about this particular bird. He wanted to know what it ate, where it roosted, how many times it blinked its eyes. Everything. It was, after all, personal.

Automatically he poured a cup of coffee, still pondering the old bird's whereabouts. The hot coffee steamed in the chilly morning air. Leaning against the van, he sipped its warm bitter liquid and schemed some more. This year he would get the old bird. Once and for all. He would get it this morning because the tom had run out of tricks. The hunter now knew them all.

He would set up just down the creek from the big sycamore. He would slip in quietly, stake out a hen decoy and then hunker down against a good-sized oak by the creek bank. This time the old bird would be his. It would fly down as usual and come strutting down the creek bank as usual. And the hunter would be there to greet him. As simple as that.

The man felt smug as he stood in the dark. He had finally figured out that old bird. No more surprises. No more twists and turns. No more mess-ups.

He had finally figured out that old bird. For starters, he was wise to its peculiar habits – that the tom did not go up ridges in the morning, as most birds were apt to do. One hen or one hundred hens on the ridge, it didn't matter. This old bird did not go up a ridge until after the legal shooting hour was over – noon. Not ever.

But, in the afternoon, like clockwork, it bopped up the ride and made quite a fuss. Most hunters who scouted it – and there were legions – naturally found it at the top of the ridge. The bird gobbled from up there in a heartbeat. And talk about turkey sign? Why that rascal had practically tore the place up, scratching, eating and strutting. Come sunset, it would gobble once and then beat a hasty retreat down the ridge to roost in the sycamore by the creek, leaving most hunters assuming it had roosted on the ridge. It was a sneaky bird.

When most folks returned the next morning to the hunt the old tom, it would gobble and gobble and gobble, all morning long. But, not from the ridge. The gobbles would come from the hollow below and the bird would not budge from the creek bed. It would strut up and down that bottom. It would walk a path right up through the thickest tangles you'd ever seen. It would throw its voice, bouncing it off the opposite ridge to make hunters think it was somewhere else. And it worked.

To make matters worse, the old bird would slip up the side of the ridge just a little, enough to make you think it was coming in. And just when you'd get excited and raise your gun, it would slip back down the hill, gobbling all the way to the creek bottom and safety.

Yup, it was personal. The old bird was a rascal of the first order.

Unfortunately, it took the hunter six mornings to figure out most of this foolishness. Sadly, the sixth morning came after the season was over and he had replaced his shotgun with a camera. However, thank goodness, he now had its number and he was going to even the score. He had waited all year for another chance. And like the joke punch line said, "today's the day." Today was the day, the hunter's day. "Enough thinking," he mumbled to himself. "It is time to hunt."

The man flung the last dregs of coffee on the ground, tossed the cup into the van, geared up and headed for the hollow. He knew the hollow as well as his own bedroom in the dark. It had become his second home almost. He moved quickly and quietly, the dew drenched his pants.

He reached the set-up spot, a large oak in the creek bottom and eased into position. He staked out the hen decoy, about 20 yards behind him and along side the creek in an open spot. The old tom would look past him and focus on the fake bird instead as it strutted its stuff down the path.

The man sat down beside the oak, legs bent, heels dug into the leaves and earth. He had clipped enough leafy branches to poke them into the ground and hide his position. He could see up and down the creek clearly. The old bird would come from his right. The set-up was perfect. All he had to do was wait now. Send a few soft "boinky boink" calls from his Jet Slate to the bird in the sycamore when the time was right.

The hunter did not have to wait very long. The songbirds flitted past and chirped as the new day dawned. Then, the gobble, a glorious gobble shattered the morning stillness. The old tom was at home in the sycamore tree and ready to tango again. After several more gobbles, the hunter sweetly called back. Two "boinky boinks". Two soft yelps. Then he slipped the call into his pocket. It took two to tango and he had made his reply.

The old tom double-gobbled back at the sparse calls. A loud commotion in the tree leaves followed and the longbeard was on the ground. And on its way down the creek bottom.

Look out! The tom gobbled again. The man waited, nerves steady, gun ready and pointing in the bird's direction. The tom gobbled again and appeared on the path. The hunter had him dead in his sights. Twenty paces. Nerves of steel. He tried to ignore the mosquito buzzing in his ear.

"*Bizzzzzzzzzz, bizzzzzzzzz, bizzzzzzzzz.*"

An annoying mosquito-like buzz woke the hunter up. His travel clock's reliable alarm. In the distance, a lonesome freight train rumbled its way north, horn wailing every minute or so. He sat up in the back of his van, rubbing his eyes, body stiff from sleeping on the hard floor.

He had been dreaming about turkeys again. He leaned against the front seat and tried to remember the dream. He could not. He groped for his glasses and flashlight. It was 5 a.m., opening day of spring turkey season. His mind turned to more important things – revenge.

Then it hit him, all of a sudden, a ton of bricks, a sack of hammers. The alarm. The train. He had been there before. He had done this before. Déjà vu.

Or worse.

Ground Hog Day! ↓↓

A dandy Cass County, Illinois, gobbler struts his stuff for Chris Young, outdoor writer and photographer for the Springfield State Journal Register. Photograph courtesy of the State Journal Register and Chris Young.

Chapter Eight

"Ghillie Suits & Seat Cushions"
More Gadgets & Gizmos

In my heyday as an outdoor writer at the Dayton Daily News and editor of Barron's Outdoor Guide magazine, folks sent me all sorts and conditions of new outdoor products to test. One such fellow from Virginia sent me a ghillie suit to try out. And I did. Opening day, spring season, in Chautauqua County, New York.

I forget the year but it was a long time ago and way before ghillie suits were available in the catalogs. Today, every outdoor catalog features at least one model of the bushy suit. But, 10 or more years ago, only military snipers knew about them and used them. No self-respecting turkey hunter worth his weight in Quaker Boy Boss

Hens would dare show up rigged out in one of these outfits.

Except, of course, me. Because I have no shame. And I was a cheap date, according to my wife.

Well, lo and behold, I arrived in the middle of the night at Art Kibbe's house, the night before opening day. I sneaked into the house under the cover of darkness and climbed the stairs to my bedroom for a short four-hour nap before Art woke me up. In my duffle bag, the new ghillie suit awaited. I was a tad bit embarrassed to let anyone see it before the time was right. Before it was too late to get talked out of using it.

All things considered, the ghillie suit has a fine and distinquished history in the hunting tradition. In the old country, gamekeepers, otherwise known as ghillies, would wear them to hide and catch poachers on the lord's estate. They made them from tattered rags and sacks. And the suits provided perfect camouflage. Many a poacher was fooled and apprehended by the ghillie hiding in the bush while wearing his suit.

The military adopted this camouflage suit in World War I. I remember watching a History Channel special on snipers and seeing British soldiers wearing the suit. But, if you wish to differ, go right ahead. It's your dollar.

The first suits were constructed with burlap strips torn from sacks, dyed various forest colors and attached to a parka body. The burlap strips were fuzzy and matched the foliage and the flora of the terrain.

Well, I tossed the burlap get-up into the truck bed as we departed the house and donned it in the dark after we parked the truck on Art's farm near Gobbler Corner.

Gobbler Corner – a one-in-a-million spot that attracted turkeys every spring.

Art finally spied the outfit, broke out in big grin and said I looked like Alley Oop, the caveman cartoon character. And I did. What with the bushy leggings, humped up shoulders and mop-top head piece. I said thanks. I proceeded to explain what it was and how I got it. He mumbled, "Yep, I reckon so."

We headed for the log blinds in the Corner and arrived under cover of darkness. Turkeys were roosted in the trees just across the little creek that sliced the Corner in two. They did not see or hear us arrive. We sat down and waited.

The birds proceeded to fly down, after copious amounts of gobbling, and a curious hen proceeded to walk right to me. Obviously a new bush had sprouted overnight in a spot that had previously been bush-less. The hen stared at the new bush – me - for five minutes. It was not more than five yards away. I stared back, smug as a bug in a rug in a bushy suit. It finally got bored and walked away.

Next arrived a young gobbler and it gave me a close inspection, then it too departed.

Finally a great big old gobbler appeared and headed right for me. I did not permit it to get close enough for inspection. At 20 yards, I pulled the trigger on my Winchester 1300.

Ka-blam!

The bird flipped backwards, legs peddling the invisible bicycle upside down. I remained motionless, since the bird was definitely out for the count and headed to the Great Strut Zone in the Sky. The other birds, about 10 in all, froze in their tracks and stared at the bush – me. They could not believe their eyes. A bush shot Bubba! Is nothing sacred?

Soon thereafter they beat a hasty retreat down the hill and into the gas well clearing, leaving Old Bubba and the shooting bush behind.

The Alley Oop suit did not last the day, however. Before I could get up and retrieve the dead gobbler, I snorted out the loudest sneeze I have ever unleashed. It shook the trees, rattled the branches and triggered the fire siren in Gerry.

The microscopic burlap fuzz in the suit had multiplied and worked its way up my nostrils, into my eyes and on to my exposed skin. As a result, I fell into a sneezing fit of epileptic proportions and lapsed into an itching seizure of horrendous magnitude. My God, I was allergic to the suit! I soon realized that it would be of little use if I could not control the sneezing and irritation.

Looking like a bush is one thing. But, a sneezing bush that scratches itself incessantly would certainly blow the deal and scatter the turkeys.

Hence, the first problem with the burlap ghillie suit became evident - the proliferation of fuzz and sneezing and the itching frenzy that ensued. The second problem was similar to the cow silhouette situation, which I have mentioned in previous books.

Once the word got out that there was a bush inhabiting Gobbler Corner that could shoot turkeys, nary a turkey worth its weight in Silver Queen slates, would get within a stone's throw. Turkeys wise up pretty fast and the news of a shooting bush would travel. I say again, trouble rides a fast horse.

As to the future of the ghillie suit, I did what I always do with new products – turkey vest with the pack frame in it, calls of dubious and specious nature, gadgets and gizmos, etc. I gave it to my son, the Army officer! I figured he would know what to do with it even though he is an armor officer.

I phoned him later to see how the suit worked and to see if he was allergic to it as I was. He explained that you have to wash the suit first before you put it on! A couple of trips in the washer eliminated the fuzz and he proceeded to fool several Texas Rios. Who knew?

To the best of my recollections, I do believe he still owns the suit but I am not sure that he uses it. And, since I don't want it back, I am not going to ask him either!

I shall conclude this chapter with some remarks about my world famous turkey collection – seat cushions. I have already elucidated, illuminated and otherwise pontificated about my turkey vest collection in a previous book, *Bend Over Here It Comes!* Chapter Five. Gadgets and gizmos.

Forsooth, I have another collection. Turkey seat cushions. Since I suffer from a terminal (pun intended) and genetic case of *gluteus minimus* – a bony ass – seat cushions are an essential accoutrement for turkey hunting.

Over the years I have managed to obtain dozens of various and sundry makes and models. I even have a couple of home-made jobbies that my wife and I whipped up. If memory serves me, my first seat cushion was a wafer-thin excuse that came with my first turkey vest. It was about as comfortable as a folded newspaper. I deep-sixed it after one day of painful sitting and attempted hunting.

Next, I purchased a hard-foam seat from K-Mart. It was a tad more comfortable but not much. I inserted it into the wafer thin seat pocket and along side the wafer seat but to no avail. It now resides in the gizmo chest.

My third seat cushion was home-made. It was generous. Large dimensions, two-inch thick foam and covered in brand new Trebark camo. It lasted until the first day it rained. Two inches of upholstery foam will soak up 10 gallons of rain water and weigh 40 pounds. It resides next to the hard foam seat in the chest.

My fourth cushion was the one made for deer hunters and filled with foam pellets that heat up. A hot seat is not a good idea in the spring time. Plus, a pesky root poked a hole in it and I had a heck of a time picking up the little foam pellets. All two thousand. It lives in the seat chest, too. With duct tape over the hole.

Cushion Number Five. I could not resist. HS Strut introduced the inflatable seat and I rushed to the store to buy one. It was self-inflating but I soon discovered that blowing extra air into it fatten it to a more desirable thickness. The first time I used it, I blew it up, slipped it under my bony butt and sat down contented.

Kerwhoosh! It exploded! The self-inflating valve blew its gasket and I was left sitting on a piece of rubber, flat as a pancake.

I returned the product to the store and told the salesperson that I thought there was something wrong with it. I explained what had happened, intelligently omitting the "user error" – blowing the darn thing up. The salesperson did not blink his eye. He told me to go pick out another one and I did.

Cushion Six B, as it is now classified, worked just fine as long as I refrained from adding extra inflation. However, there was one day in Texas, while hunting with my son, when the nozzle got caught in another tenacious root and snapped right off.

Kerwhoosh!

I had heard that sound before and knew my butt would be on terra firma fast. Six B could not be returned to the store because human error was evident. I stashed it in the cushion chest for old times sake and a possible valve implant when the technology catches up.

Number Seven was suppose to be the lucky number. It was self-inflating and triangular in shape and big. I saw it at WalMart and could not resist. It lasted one day. The internal backflow valve had a slow leak. I did not have the heart to return it to the store. Instead, I saved it and loan it to hunters that I am obligated to take hunting, once. I love the look on their faces when they have to sit still for long periods of time and their butts eventually sink to the hard ground.

My eighth, ninth and tenth cushions came attached to turkey vests and were sub-par. Again, too thin, too flimsy. Thus, I unzipped them and tossed them into the chest. They are there in case I need to re-attach them to the vests. Serious vest collectors are pretty picky about things such as that.

Cushion 11. Seven come eleven. This cushion is a two-piece jobbie and functions fairly well as a seat. I use it more in my canoe and kayak, when I get the notion to duck hunt, than I do turkey hunting. However, the seat bottom is thick and comfortable. The back tends to get in the way more often than not. Cushion 11 remains in active service. My buddy, Bobby Dale, also uses a Number 11 seat cushion so they can't be that bad.

Numero 12 is, for all intents and purposes, not strictly a seat cushion. It is a chair. One of those engineering marvels that folds up into a carry sack. It is camouflaged and I bought it at Sam's for less than 15 bucks. I tote it everywhere and hunt out of it every chance I get.

The first time I used it, I sat for an entire day in the bushes beside an alfalfa field, opening day of fall turkey season in Illinois. When I include one of my foam cushions in the seat bottom, I can sit for days in sweet comfort. I even bought Doc Lucky one of these chairs so that we would match on our hunting trips!

Since I prefer to hunt out of a ground blind, a spacious Eastman pop-up, these days, and whenever I can, the folding chair is the pinnacle of luxury. I can sit in my blind, sip my coffee, read a book, nap, call and shoot turkeys in total comfort. I have arrived in turkey hunting heaven so leave me alone. I have also converted my buddy, Bob Gowen, to the virtues of the full-size folding hunting chair. When he hunts with me, he uses my spare chair and falls sound to sleep. As far as I can tell, his snoring does not bother the turkeys.

I guess I will continue to collect turkey seats. My next-to-newest vest, Number Seven, with 22 ergos and nomics, sported an attached seat that was semi-comfortable. I did like the magnetic catches on the back that hold it in place. However, do not unzip the seat and depend on the magnets alone. An errant branch dislocated the seat in Illinois on a spring hunt in Brown County and I had to waste time, backtracking to find it.

A seat-less vest and a vest-less seat depreciate in value.

I have since deposited Number Seven in the gizmo chest because I bought one of those leafy jobbies at Bass Pro outside of Knoxville last year on my way to Brown County, Illinois. The sales lady told me that the leafy vest was their Number One seller and they had re-ordered them three times. Sadly, the seat is too thin but it does stay firmly attached when I am walking through the woods. I will continue to wear Number Eight until I find a better one. My son, Heath, bought a

Primos vest at Cabela's in Kansas City and it features a super thick and solid seat. I am tempted to buy one, too, but I will hold off until Primos adds leafy stuff to the fat-seat vest.

While at Cabela's with my son last year, I had the chance to sit in of their "Gobbler Lounger" seats. It is one of those engineering fold-up marvels and sits very low to the ground. My buddy, Terry Corder, from South Carolina swears by them so I could not help but buy it. I hunted Kansas longbeards for a week and gave the new seat a thorough field test. It passed with flying colors. However, it does have one serious, almost fatal flaw. You will have to read Chapter 14 to find out what the flaw is.

I reckon one of these days, Bill Jones from Sea Island, Georgia is going to hear about my vest and seat collection and offer me big bucks for them. Bill is the fellow who purchased part of Parker Whedon's turkey call collection for a tidy sum and some change. He also bought the late Earl Mikel's turkey call collection for a handsome figure and a small European country.

Seat cushions and turkey vests are next in line for collectables. They will appreciate over time. Mark my word. It is inevitable.

At least that is what I tell my wife every time I buy a new one.

She acts as if she believes me. ↓↓

Bob Gowen, Ray Berryhill, Bobby Dale and Parker Whedon at Bob's White House on the farm in Halifax, North Carolina. 2007 Spring Turkey Season.

    Every year Bob hosts a gathering of infamous turkey hunters, book authors and call makers at his beautiful farm on the historic Roanoke River. Bobby has written two books on turkey hunting and is well-known in his home state of Mississippi. Ray and his buddy, Scott Blanton, have written several books on Neil Cost and his turkeys calls. Their latest book is about hunting the oscellated turkey. Ray is also famous in turkey hunting circles and is Assistant Athletic Director at Mississippi State University.

    Parker is North Carolina's senior and foremost turkey hunter. He organized the first state turkey hunter association and his wing bone calls are prized among collectors. ↓↓

Chapter Nine

"Chester Departs Dodge"
Ray Berryhill & Bobby Dale Hunt in NC

As a rule, I prefer not to give gobblers a name. I prefer to shoot anonymous turkeys, birds that gobble, fly down, come running in and meet my Nitro loads before they know what hit them. On the other hand, I do make exceptions. Particularly when I have saved a tough old gobbler for a friend. What follows is a classic tale that will dog Ray Berryhill all the days of his turkey-hunting life.

Rudy Simone, Neuse NWTF chapter president, and I were scouting turkeys before the 2007 spring season. One morning we watched a tall skinny gobbler limp across a distant field at a friend's farm on the White Oak River. We got excited because the bird sported a paintbrush beard and loomed large in the binoculars. The idea of saving this bird, which we named "Chester" for Ray Berryhill, co-author of the Neil Cost books and good friend from Mississippi, popped into my mind immediately. Rudy agreed. "Chester" would be Ray's celebrity turkey when he and Bobby Dale, another good friend and book author from Mississippi, visited us to hunt the first week of the North Carolina spring season on the White Oak River.

When I got home that evening, I called Ray and left a message on his answering machine.

"Ray, we have located the perfect turkey just for you!" I exclaimed. "Since you have a proclivity to hunt and miss, I might add, handicap gobblers, Rudy and I watched an old gobbler, with a pronounced limp, travel across a friend's field this morning. We have named him, Chester, in honor of Matt Dillon's stiff-legged sidekick from the Gunsmoke TV show. Can't wait for you and Bobby to get here and for you to chase Chester. By the way, the odds are 5 to 1 on Chester."

As Sherlock Holmes would say, "The game was afoot!" Moreover, it was Ray's doing in the first place.

You see, Ray, Bobby Dale, Bob Gowen and I had shared a booth, where we sold books and turkey belts, at the 2007 NWTF National Convention in Nashville, Tennessee. We also stayed at the same motel, thanks to Bobby's recommendation. Naturally, we got to be good friends and really enjoyed our time together. Especially, happy hour.

We would gather in our room each evening after the vendor hours were over at the convention. My assistant, chauffeur and brother-in-law, Big Doug, was there, too. We would re-hash the day's events and tell tall turkey tales whilst we imbibed in our favorite liquid refreshments prior to going out for supper.

On one such evening, Ray, who is a rather gregarious fellow and who has turkey hunted in at least 25 different states, graced upon us a rather tall and humorous tale where he had shot and missed a big, fat, one-legged gobbler while hunting in Wisconsin.

Ray recollected that he must have gotten sassy, maybe a bit cocky, and figured a one-legged gobbler was no match for his savvy and finely honed turkey-killing skills. He assumed that the bird couldn't run so he calmly watched it strut into range, using one of its wings as a crutch. Little did he realize that a one-legged gobbler survives the wilds of Cheese Land by compensating for its disability. The gobbler in question could not walk, only hop. Thus, it was easy prey.

However. The gimp gobbler had an ace up its sleeve. The sucker could FLY like a bat out of hell!

In addition, it proceeded to demonstrate this amazing speed and blazing quickness by taking off like a rocket when it saw Ray move his shotgun. Ray said the bird did not land until it crossed into Minnesota.

Thus, it was Ray's destiny to challenge Chester. It was meant to be.

When the convention was over, Bob Gowen, with his gracious generosity and humble hospitality, invited the Mississippi boys to come visit us in North Carolina and hunt our turkeys. I offered to host Bobby and Ray, first, and chase turkeys along the historic White Oak River. We would hunt some very special haunts, where the old "Kurnel" Simon Everett, himself, hunted. Everett wrote about his turkey exploits in *Tales of Wild Turkey Hunting*, published in 1928. This is one of the oldest books written about turkey hunting and reprints are available from Lovett Williams's website.

Then, after a couple days of chasing the pure wild turkeys in my neck of the woods, the swamps and freshets of eastern North Carolina, we would head to Halifax County and the even more historic Roanoke River and chase turkeys that are even more wild on Bob Gowen's river bottom farm.

When spring turkey season rolled around, I picked the boys up at the airport in Raleigh and chauffeured them down to Jacksonville, whereupon we commenced to hunt Simon Everett's turkeys. I asked Rudy Simone, who lives near the White Oak River to guide Ray, whilst I guided Bobby. Rudy was more than willing to help out.

Several years back, Rudy had help guide the late Earl Mikel, author of several books about turkey calls and their makers, on his quest of killing a turkey in all 49 states. (Alaska does not have any wild turkeys.)

Furthermore, it was Ray Berryhill who inspired Earl to embark on his quest, in the first place! What comes around goes around.

While Ray and Rudy messed with Chester, Bobby Dale and I would head for the back end of the farm, which bordered the river and its prodigious swamp.

On the first morning of the hunt, I dropped Ray off at the front of the farm with Rudy and they proceeded to set up on a small field that was about 150 yards from Chester's roost tree. Since Chester was fond of the field, we figured that he would visit it sooner or later. And he did.

Meanwhile, Bobby and I headed for the field at the back of the farm. We parked the Jeep, geared up and walked quietly across the sandy corn stubble field. When we reached my favorite set up spot, we settled down beside two old and stately sycamore trees to wait for the gobblers to wake up in the nearby swamp and announced their presence. When it got light enough, Bobby noticed several large tracks in the sandy soil, directly in front of us.

"Hey, Bill?" Bobby inquired. "What kind of tracks are these?"

"Bear," I answered matter-of-factly.

"What? Bear? Are you serious?" followed Bobby.

"Yep," I answered. "We got bear. Lots of them. In fact, we got more down here than they do up in the mountains."

"I don't think I have had the pleasure of hunting turkeys in bear country before," said Bobby.

"Well, in that case," said I. "I need to tell you about the bear drill. What we do in case we encounter a bear. And, by the way, we got two bears in this case. One big set of tracks. Momma bear. One small set of tracks. Baby bear."

By this time, Bobby's eyes were getting bigger and I definitely had his attention.

"OK. The bear drill. This is what we are going to do in case we bump into those two bears. Pay close attention," I instructed.

"First of all, if we should run into these bears, we need to freeze in our tracks. Don't panic, just stop and don't move.

"Next," I continued, "I will hand you my shotgun, OK?"

"Right," said Bobby.

"After you take my shotgun, I am going to run like heck!" I exclaimed.

"You can't outrun a bear," replied Bobby, dubiously.

"Nope, I can't. But, all I need to do is run faster than you, with you loaded down with shotguns."

Needless to say, Bobby saw lots of bear tracks during our two days of turkey hunting. In fact, we saw bear tracks around every field on the farm, many more tracks than I had seen the previous season. From the number of fresh tracks and piles of bear poop, it is a wonder that we did not bump into the bears and have to initiate the bear drill during our two-day hunt.

While we were hunkered down at the river end of the farm and trying to call turkeys out of the swamp with the wind blowing 40 miles an hour, Chester showed up in his favorite field, mid-morning, where Rudy and Ray were waiting.

It was an unusually cold and windy day for April. A cold front had arrived the night before and along with it came a blustery northwest wind - gusts up to 50 miles an hour and a steady wind around 30. We dubbed this adverse weather "Hurricane Bobby-Ray" in honor of our guests.

Hunting turkeys in Hurricane Bobby-Ray was difficult at best, impossible at worst. The wind roared over our heads with the noise of a jet plane. The turkeys, which were much smarter than the hunters were, stuck to the swamps and low land and did not venture out into the fields most of the day.

At noon, we rendezvoused at the old cabin near Chester's field to compare morning notes and strategize for the afternoon hunt. Next, we drove into Maysville and had lunch at Andy's, then headed back to the farm for more hunting.

Bobby and I moved to the middle of the farm where a thick stand of pine trees at our backs would break the fierce northwest wind. We would hunt the farmer's 10-acre winter wheat field while Rudy and Ray went after Chester again. The gimp gobbler had flown into their little field that morning and stood for an hour, sunning himself and staying out of the cold wind. The boys could not coax him into gun range and they tried their best.

I suggested to Ray that he sit underneath a certain Magnolia tree next to the sandy road that came out of the Mulberry Creek swamp and try to coax Chester out. I figured Ray could find the tree easily. He was, after all, from the "Magnolia" State. Old Chester was famous for spending his afternoons, loafing in the swamp. Then, he would limp back up the sandy road towards his roost tree in the late afternoon. Ray approved of the strategy.

Bobby and I split up at the wheat field. I left Bobby at the edge of the pine trees, whilst I slipped over to the cabbage patch on the other side of the field. I had watched several gobblers and hens visit that patch frequently in the afternoon. Plus, birds often came out of another beaver swamp to the north, crossed a grassy field, and loafed around the winter wheat field and pine trees in the afternoon. Bobby was in a great spot to shoot a turkey.

Not long after I had settled in at the cabbage patch – wind still howling over my head

– did I watch four gobblers exit the beaver swamp and head for Bobby. The problem was that the birds would arrive from behind Bobby and he would not have a clue. Thus, I quickly departed the patch and headed back to Bobby to warn him. Just as I arrived, the gobblers appeared in the grassy field to Bobby's left about 100 yards away. It turned out that the gobblers were Jakes so we watched them with curiosity.

Periodically, we would call as loudly as possible. Bobby with his paddle box and me with a diaphragm call. As soon as the notes reached the strong wind above the pine tree windbreak, they vanished. Furthermore, every now and then one of the jakes would gobble – thrust out its neck and shake – but no sound erupted. Although we were close enough to hear the gobble, again, the wind snatched it away. We finally quit calling and went to watching the birds.

It did not take them long to make a beeline for the cabbage patch. I thought to myself no big deal. I would rather sit with Bobby and visit than shoot a young gobbler at the cabbage patch. However, no good deed goes unpunished.

While the shortbeards picked at the tender young cabbage shoots poking out of the ground, two adult gobblers charged out of the swamp and ran full speed to the patch. They commenced to puff up and bully the young gobblers. I now thought to myself, dang, if I had stayed on that patch, I would have killed one of those longbeards.

About this time, we faintly heard a shot towards the front of the farm – Chester's territory. A few minutes later, Rudy's voice squawked over the walkie-talkie I carried in my vest.

"Gobble, gobble no more. Chester is dead. Long live Chester."

Bobby and I exchanged smiles, figured Ray had beaten the odds and finally dispatched a handicap gobbler. I then suggested to Bobby that we put the sneak on the cabbage patch and he agreed. We slipped out of the pine trees, bent over and commenced to what I call the "Indian run" through the knee-high wheat field. It was a sight to see. Two old men closing in on 60 years of age bent over and dashing through the wheat.

We were able to reach the fencerow between the wheat and cabbage patch without being seen. However, when we poked our heads up and around the fencerow trees, the turkeys had already drifted away from the patch and into a broom straw field. We stood and watched their heads poke out of the straw like periscopes on a submarine. We tried some more calling but the roaring wind defeated the purpose. Before long, the birds exited the field and vanished back into the swamp. Our hunt was over.

Forsooth, we headed back to the Jeep, walking around the perimeter of the wheat field and admiring the plentitude of bear tracks and poop. Once we reached the vehicle, we drove back to the old cabin to find Rudy and Ray.

When we arrived, they were waiting, big grins on their faces.

Ray had indeed shot Chester.

The old bird had limped out of the swamp, up the sandy road and into a load of Ray's pellets.

Old Chester was a typical swamp turkey, tall and slender, with long legs and dark wing feathers. Henry Davis, author of the *American Wild Turkey*, would have been pleased. It was a classic purebred low-country wild turkey. No domestic genes in its pool. It sported a thick 12-inch beard and hooked spurs, at least one-and-a-half inches long. But, alas, it weighed only 11 pounds. A tad on the light side.

We all agreed that Chester was on its last legs, pun intended, and Ray had put the poor bird out of its misery.

When we retuned to my house that evening, Bobby, being an ER physician, did a post mortem on the crippled leg and discovered that it had broken at the knee joint and the two bones had fused together. Thus, Chester suffered from severe arthritis and would have not survived another winter in the wild.

It is Bob's and my turn to hunt with the Mississippi boys on their turf next spring. I reckon a get-even surprise will be part of the package. Bobby has a reputation for passing off barbecued raccoon as pork ribs to visiting turkey hunters.

As for Ray and his tendency to chase handicap turkeys, I think we cured him of this ailment.

Once and for all. ↓↓

Bill, Chester, Ray and Rudy. Chester has the appropriate NC handicap placard dangling from his wing. Take note of the paintbrush beard, hanging down from his breast. No doubt, Chester ruled the roost in his heyday when he was short of tooth and long of breath.

Chapter Ten

"The Power of Stink"
To stink or not to stink. That is the question.

The late Henry Davis, an attorney in Florence, South Carolina, wrote *The American Wild Turkey* in 1949. In it he remarked, "Indeed, if the wild gobbler were endowed with the sense of smell to the same degree that he possesses the senses of sight and hearing, he would be more than a match for any of his foes. A shotgun would be practically useless in hunting such quarry and nothing but a long-range rifle could be relied on to bring him to bag." Page 49.

It is a good thing that turkeys cannot smell as well as deer. With their superb eyesight and acute hearing, we would find it impossible to hunt them. Even worse, someone would make a billion dollars selling turkey stink products, too.

I am still unsold, unconverted and otherwise skeptical about deer stink products. I have several deer hunting buddies who swear by them. They tote large pharmacies of stink and non-stink products with them on their deer hunts. I am afraid to ask how much money they have spent. I, on the other hand, prefer to stink. It is much less expensive. I do take showers on a regular and persistent basis. Not just Saturday nights.

However, I do have a tendency to slack off on personal hygiene while I am turkey hunting. In other words, I don't shower, brush my teeth or shave every day. Heck, half the fun of being away from home on a hunting or fishing trip is letting yourself go to seed, ripen and blossom. I have this one hunting buddy – I will omit his name lest he decide to quit going with me – who showers every morning BEFORE we go turkey hunting.

Somone once joked that Virginia gentlemen wash their hands BEFORE and after they visit the men's restroom. But, my clean buddy is not from Virginia nor has he traveled farther east than Indianapolis.

I, on the other hand, avoid bathing rituals until the last day of the hunt. Then I shower, brush and shave lest my wife refuse me entrance upon return home. Normally, I change my underwear each day while hunting and fishing.

However, I have discovered that it can be good luck to wear the same pair over and over. For example, in Boston, baseball fans do not change socks in the middle of a World Series. I reckon clothing stores lost money in 2004.

Forsooth, the next time you leave home on a hunting trip and you have trouble shooting a turkey, it could very well be that your underwear is causing the bad luck. Either change them or stop changing them, whatever the case may be. You can thank me later for this secret tip.

I discovered this cosmological clothing secret long ago on a hunting trip to Chautauqua County, New York. I had packed in a hurry as I am wont to do and completely forgot to include underwear in the duffel bag. Thus, I discovered a day or two, maybe three, into the hunt that I did not have any Fruit of the Loom. My luck had headed south and I figured it was time to change U-trou. Art and I dashed over to the K-Mart in Fredonia and I purchased a six-pack of briefs.

I shot a big, fat old gobbler the very next morning and I was sporting a crisp, new pair of underwear. There you go.

Back to stink. If I had a dollar for every deer that has walked by me, up to me, around me and behind me while hunting *au naturel* - without non-stink products - I could buy three or four heavy-duty freezers to store all the venison. I have had deer walk, swim, run, hop, skip and jump right into gun range each and every hunting season of my life. Not once, but several times a season. If I were a subsistence hunter I could have fed the family well on deer meat.

Since I did not attend the School of Stink, why do deer come so close to me? Perhaps, it is my pleasing personality? Or personal magnetism? Or perhaps, I just don't stink. Except when I eat garlic. Italian food. I had a friend in high school who swore he did not stink. Or sweat. He did not use deodorent. To the best of my recollection, he did not stink. He attributed his lack of odor to "mind over matter". He swore that he could control his sweating and aroma. Whatever. He ended up dating my ex-girlfriend later in college. Which was the last time I saw both of them. Stink or no stink.

Back to subsistence hunting. In hindsight, I probably missed a great opportunity to supplement our meager food budget in my early years of preaching. Since preachers are suppose to be "spiritual" people and have few material needs, most are not paid well. Not even close. After all, they only work on Sunday, right?

They are expected to sit at home, wrapped up in a used blanket, read the Bible, fast, pray and not complain. If they have wives and children, and we are more comfortable with that arrangement than with Adam and Steve, the rest of the family is suppose to ignore their material needs, share blankets, read the Bible, fast, pray and not complain, too.

Because of that financial reality, I supplemented my paltry preacher pay by moonlighting. In the early days, I worked every Saturday (I only got one day off a week) with a buddy, cutting, hauling and selling firewood. I cut enough wood to help heat our house as well. Next, I took on a second career - taxidermy. I set up shop in the basement and mounted ducks, pheasants, dove and quail for the local hunters. Back in those days they paid me $25 to stuff a duck. Cash on the barrel head. That extra money made a big difference at Christmas, birthdays, doctors' visits and paying for Ampicillin, the liquid gold antibiotic prescribed to our three children on a regular, persistent and pricey basis.

I remember a parishioner once asked me how I learned to do taxidermy. I answered her, "Reform School". I did not attend reform school but I enjoyed the look of shock and disbelief when I told folks that I did. I guess the Devil made me do it.

In 1978 I met Duane Raver, the editor of NC Wildlife magazine, at a local hunting club supper. My wood-cutting buddy was a member of the club and took me to the dinner as his guest. Furthermore, he suggested to Duane that I write a story about fly-fishing and Duane publish it. Forsooth, I did. A story about fly-fishing in the mountains. The pay was $78. Easy to remember.

I thereupon reduced my wood cutting and increased my outdoor writing. And the food, clothing and medicine budget increased. For the past 30 years, I have moonlighted in various and sundry outdoor writing capacities in order to supplement, augment and amplify my ministerial wages. I am not complaining. No sour grapes. Actually, as I see it, I am most fortunate to have had a second and third trade to ply now that I am retired and free to hunt and fish on Sundays.

    I am officially retired from preaching and getting paid by the pension fund to stay away from church. Verily. Before I could receive my pension benefits, I had to sign a certified document that swore I would not work at church, full-time, again. Which is a nice situation, if you think about it. It does not make much sense to retire and then work full-time in the same job. But, I reckon some preachers try to double dip. Otherwise, why the need to sign an official document?

    I recently informed my saintly wife, mischievously, of course, that according to official church rules, I only have to go to church three times a year to be considered an active communicant. I am not making this rule up. It really exists. In fact, the number was recently raised from two to three! My plan, therefore, was to go church the first three Sundays in January of each year and hunt and fish the rest of the year.

    The plan sounded good to me but she did not buy it. Using church math, I figured I have accumulated more than enough church attendance to cover at least three lifetimes, maybe more. Let's see, twice on Sundays, once on Wednesdays, hundreds of weddings, funerals and special worship gatherings times 32 years.

Vestry (church council) meetings are worth 100 extra points a piece. Yep, I reckon I have a sufficient number of church attendances in case my barns burn over night. But, discretion being the better part of valor and Mickey being a Mouse, I did not share this church math with my spouse. I knew I was treading on thin ice and heading for the frigid water.

Moving on. Retirement, with or without church, means finally having time to write books and chase turkeys with my friends all over the country. I will do some taxidermy on a few big gobblers, when I feel like it. Make some wingbone and box calls, when the spirit moves. Read more books on turkey hunting. I will not put off the things I want to do any longer. My father did that and things did not work out.

"When I retire," he often said to me, "I am going to fish every day. Rain or shine. Hot or cold. I am going to do all the things I have wanted to do and have had to put off."

He retired and fished for a couple of years. Then he was diagnosed with prostate cancer. He recovered from the cancer, twice. He also struggled with severe lung damage that had developed over the years from breathing toxic chemicals in his textile plants. He spent much of his retirement in poor health and was not able to do many of the activities that he had postponed until retirement.

Back in my meager pre-retirement days, I was a lean, mean hunting machine. Shotgun shells were 10 to 20 cents a piece, depending upon the load, and I supplemented our groceries as much as possible with dove, quail, grouse and ducks. I was interested in learning how to turkey hunt and considered traveling to Camp Lejeune or the Uwharrie Forest to give it a try. But, I did not get around to it.

According to NC Wildlife Commission records, we had about 2,000 wild turkeys all total back then. The turkey season was in the fall. Wild turkeys were considered "upland game". Because my local counties, Cumberland County, first, and then Hertford County, later, were closed to turkey hunting and I did not know any turkey hunters, who could teach me the skills, I stuck to the traditional upland birds, waterfowl and fishing to increase the family groceries. I would have hunted turkeys if we had had them close by and an open season.

Anyway, when I reminisce on those lean early years, I think maybe I should have shot every deer that I could have, legally and in season, of course. The game and opportunities were plentiful. Obviously, I did not stink back then. Nor did the deer smell me. The only attractant that deer hunters used back in those days was Mott's apple juice. They splashed it on like after shave. And they never washed their hunting clothes. Whatever the reasons, I forget now, I did not hunt deer much, only a time or two. I also refrained from shooting them while hunting other critters.

Be that as it may, I could have shot a lot of deer if I had wanted to. Stink or no stink. Moreover, since I have hunted turkeys, going on 25 years, I could have piled on the venison as well. With bow and gun and rifle.

A couple years back, I had a chance to shoot a massive central Illinois 8-point buck – such as the ones you drool over on TV - on my last turkey bow hunt in Cass County. I passed the shot because I was hunting turkeys. AND, I was smoking a cheap cigar that afternoon while painfully standing and sitting in a 12-foot ladder stand. The buck walked out of the woods and into the field in front me at 30 yards and stood there!

Thirty minutes later, I proceeded to call in three longbeards and shoot a fat one – which was my original purpose – while the buck munched away in the middle of the alfalfa field. I made the mistake of telling Doc Lucky about the buck and before I could return to shoot it, he slipped in to the woods the next day and put an arrow through its heart.

If I had been a subsistence sort of guy, I would have busted that buck at 30 yards, waited for the gobblers to arrive, whacked one of those, too, and headed home with venison and turkey meat.

However, the point is I am unsold on the power of stink. My mind is open and I could be convinced otherwise. But, the jury is still out and inclinating towards *nolo contendere*.

While I am postulating on the senses, I should mention that I have read in the piles of turkey books that I own that turkey eyesight is mighty powerful. Several writers have claimed that it is ten times more powerful than human sight. Be that as it may, I decided to experiment to see if this made any sense.

One lazy fall afternoon, while I was relaxing in the soft, dry leaves on the bank of a hill in Chautauqua County and waiting with Art Kibbe for a fall flock to return to roost, I got to thinking about that 10X eyesight of turkeys. I just happened to have with me at the time a small pair of 10X field glasses. So, I foraged around in my vest, snagged the glasses and proceeded to test the theory.

I raised the field glasses to my eyes, focused them and began to glass the woods below me. I figured this must be how turkeys see things. Sort of.

After a short time I began to get accustomed to the telescopic field of vision and began to see all sorts and conditions of woodland life that my naked eye had missed. Before long, I detected some movement, which turned out to be two deer – does browsing along with no clue I was watching them. I watched them for several minutes as they moved quietly through the forest, nipping a bud here, crunching an acorn or two there.

After an hour or so of watching the woods via 10X vision, I pretty much got the picture. If I had that kind of vision, watch out turkeys!

Since I have limited human vision, corrected to 20-20 at that, I make up for it with an uncanny ability to detect motion, the slightest motion, in the woods. My peripheral vision is formidable.

I can sit in my Lazy Boy chair; and while reading a book, I can spot the slightest motion in the room around me. A small bug on the carpet. A fly buzzing by. At night when I am reading, I often catch a glimpse of a tiny flicker at the window next to me – a tree frog as it jumps up and sticks to the glass pane. Without raising my eyes from the book pages. It visits often because the light in the room attracts bugs to the window, a.k.a. grocery store. Thus, if you were to add 10X power to my motion-detecting wide-angle vision, a lot more turkeys would need to worry.

Anyway, back to turkey vision. What I want to know is how do the experts KNOW that a turkey can see 10 times better than humans? How did they arrive at this scientific fact? Or is it like atomic theory. An educated guess based on the apparent action and reaction of atoms. Or evolution? A theory based upon observation and deduction. Or has some wildlife biologist at N.C. State strapped a turkey in an examining chair and asked it to read the eye chart?

What I DO know is that turkey can see extremely well at what ever power they possess and it is part and parcel of the necessary equipment to stay alive in the woods when all sorts of critters are tying to eat you.

I mentioned in my last book about the time Art and Dan Kibbe and I were hunting spring turkeys at the gas well above Gobbler Corner. Art proceeded to call in an extremely wary longbeard that another hunter had scared into next week earlier in the morning. Dan saw the bird first as it warily crept ever so closer and raised his 10-gauge cannon to shoot it. The turkey stood motionless at 45 yards, gazing intently at Dan and its surroundings. When Dan dipped his head down behind the scope, the turkey flopped its wing, spun around and hightailed it out of Dodge.

Dan is an accomplished turkey hunter and is keenly aware that any movement will spook a turkey, especially a wise, old gobbler that has had its caged rattled a few hours earlier. I am sure he moved his head slowly to the scope. But, the old tom saw the movement nonetheless and departed for parts unknown.

Joe Hutto, the fanatical fellow who lived with wild turkeys, wrote in his book, *Illuminations in the Flatwoods*, that turkeys may not recognize the human hunter as a predator form, unless he stands up and starts walking. When the hunter is hunkered down and motionless, back against a tree and well-camouflaged, the turkey will still recognize this shape as odd and not belonging to the order of things. In other words, the odd shaped lump against the tree was not there yesterday. Therefore, red alert! Something ain't right. Let's get the heck out of here.

This situation sounds more like a case of photographic memory to me than ten-power eyesight. However, if you add super memory and extraordinary eyesight together you get a bird that can see you coming, sitting, standing and leaving! Empty-handed.

Final words. I will wrap this chapter up with a tribute and apology to one of my favorite performers, Huey Lewis and the News.

The power of stink is a curious thing, make a one man weep, make another man sing. Change a hawk to a little bobolink. More than a feeling that's the power of stink.

Tougher than diamonds, rich like cream, stronger and harder than a bad girl's dream. Make a bad one good, make a wrong one right. The power of stink that keeps you home at night.

You don't need money, don't take fame. Don't need no credit card to ride this train. It's strong and it's sudden and it's cruel sometimes. But it might just save your life. That's the power of stink. ↓ ↓

The author poses with Thanksgiving Dinner at Scottland in Chautauqua County, New York. Photo by Scott Forbes.

Chapter Eleven

"Turkeys Don't"
But sometimes they do. Go figure.

My long-time, long-suffering, long of tooth and short of breath mentor, Art Kibbe, from Sinclairville, New York, tells me that "the one thing that is predictable about turkeys is that they are unpredictable."

If he has told me this once, he has told me this a thousand times. If I had five dollars (inflation) for every time I have read in a how-to-hunt turkey book or heard some self-proclaimed "expert" that turkeys "don't do something" – cross fences, travel through thick brush, fly across creeks and so forth and so on – I would sitting on the front porch of my mountain cabin, rocking in a chair and sipping G&Ts instead of pinching pennies and unplugging my own toilets.

Permit me to set the record straight. **Turkeys can and do just about everything they need to do to stay alive and well!**

I have tangled with turkeys smart enough to pilot airplanes if their feet could reach the pedals. Well, almost. So, do not fool yourself into thinking otherwise. The next time you read some how-to-kill a big gobbler article in your favorite magazine and the writer tells you that turkeys don't do something. Think again and reach for the saltshaker.

For example, take the time I miraculously called an old gobbler in from clear across a creek valley only to have the dad-blasted bird climb a sheer cliff and circle in behind me.

Back during the Second World War, the Tenth Mountain Division was organized with snow-skiers and mountain guides. They trained in the States, then shipped to Italy and deployed in the Apennine mountains. Their first action was the assault on Riva Ridge, part of the Mt. Belvedere campaign.

Now the Germans occupied Riva Ridge and from that vantage point, their observation posts could direct artillery fire on the allied troops in the valley below. They, of course, left the sheer cliff face of the ridge unprotected because they thought no allied soldiers could climb it. Thus, they were safe from attack in that direction and concentrated their defenses elsewhere.

Enter the Tenth Mountain Division. During the night, the soldiers of the Tenth climbed the cliff, attacked the Germans by surprise and took the ridge.

My hunt in Wolf Creek valley turned out to be a turkey rendition of Riva Ridge. I was completely convinced that no turkey alive could ascend the sheer cliff in front of me, so I sat down against a large oak tree and faced the opposite direction. Surely, the old gobbler that had flown across the creek and valley – which was another feat that turkeys don't do - would waltz right up the gentle slope that reached down into the valley. Not exactly.

Before I could say "Holy Moly," the gobbler quickly climbed the cliff and surrounded me. I laid my gun down and whimpered into surrender. The old gobbler had obviously read the book, the WW II book.

And then there was the time that a fall flock of birds slipped through the thickest tangle of blackberry briars that could rip your pants to shreds. Art and I had roosted this bunch of birds the evening before and were in position the next morning to intercept them. We figured the one spot we did not have to worry about was the humungous thicket of briars that occupied our right flank. Forsooth, we sat in the tops of recently lumbered trees and waited for the birds to enter our field of fire.

The turkeys proceeded to fly down, gather together and march right through the briar thicket and out of gun range. We proceeded, on the other hand, to jump up and run full bore at the flock lest we scatter them and call them back in later. One problem. The briar patch was between the birds and us. And patch is an understatement.

When we hit the briar thicket, we were immediately stopped dead in our tracks. The thick briars ripped at our coats and pants, slashed us across the face and diverted our attention from turkeys to survival. We painfully disengaged from the briars and slowly backtracked to the open woods. By this time, the flock was long gone. We headed for the truck for coffee, Little Debbie cakes and to treat our wounds.

Yes, wild turkeys love thick, sharp briar thickets. And the succulent blackberries dangling from the thorny stalks.

Back down here in eastern North Carolina, the swamp daddy gobblers fly from tree to tree all morning long and bypass the ground all together! Forget about sitting against a tree, calling and waiting for a gobbler to come waltzing in. Nine times out of ten, they are more likely to fly in and land in a tree right over your head.

I learned this lesson, one fine spring morning while I was hunting on Mr. Herring's river field. It was my second spring season back home in North Carolina and I had not become thoroughly acquainted with swamp turkeys and their peculiar inclinations, tendencies and proclivities.

Forsooth, I have since learned that they will stay on their roost all morning long, especially if it is over a swamp. They will gobble their heads off, as if they were on dry land, while watching the surrounding trees and dry patches of land below for hens to arrive.

Turkeys do not always take the short route to the ground, either. Most of the time, they will roost along side a creek, some say on the north slope of the creek bank to get some protection from the wind. When it is time to fly down, they simply hop off the limb and take two seconds to glide to the bottom. No noise, no effort. My son, the Major, who has Jump Wings, calls this a controlled descent.

However, some gobblers have not gone to Ft. Benning and Jump School. They prefer to launch out of the trees and will fly long distances off the roost across creeks, rivers, wide fields and pastures. Take the time Bill Pittman and I were hunting an old tom at the Upper 125 farm in Cass County, Illinois.

Every time we left the upper pasture on the way back to work, on the way out, we noticed a rather large old gobbler strutting in the front hillside pasture. The $64,000 question was where the heck that old boy was roosting. There wasn't a roost tree within a half a mile of the pasture. How did this bird get to the front pasture so early every morning? Was it sleeping in a ground hog hole, as pheasants sometimes do?

We decided to find out.

The very next morning we arrived at the Upper 125 in the dark, parked below the front hillside pasture, hiked up the dirt road to the creek and sat down. As the eastern sky gradually grew brighter, we heard a gobbler announce its presence from the tree line at the top of a hill about a quarter mile away. I decided not to call, figuring the old bird would hop off his limb and glide to the hillside underneath it. Turkeys don't fly a half mile off the roost and land in the middle of a pasture.

After about 30 minutes of gobbling, and us watching the tree line and wondering where that old bird would go, we were amazed to see a tiny black dot rocket out of the trees and head in our direction. The dot grew larger and, lo and behold, it turned into a rather large, fat old gobbler zeroing in on the pasture in front of us. It zoomed in over our heads, like a passenger jet on approach, gear and flaps down, and Hello! The bird landed on the other side of the creek from us, right smack dab in the middle of the hillside pasture. We were stunned! A perfect two-point landing.

The gobbler then proceeded to stand at attention and survey the surroundings for at least 30 minutes without moving one muscle. We are talking turkey statue! I called to it, periodically and softly, on my little Jet Slate. It remained stolid. A Citadel cadet "braced" for parade. Chin tucked. Eyes front. No movement. Finally, it ignored us and slowly marched up the creek in the direction of the little lower pasture, where my natural ground blind was located.

We should have been sitting there that morning. If we had only known.

Another old wives tale is that turkeys don't cross fences. If I had five dollars for every time I have seen a turkey scoot under a barbed wire fence or jump up on the fence post and jump down on the other side, I would be wasting away the time in Margarita Ville with old JB, himself.

One fall season in Cass County, Illinois, I watched two different flocks of turkeys, one afternoon; take turns jumping up to a fence post and jump flopping down to the other side of the fence. I was sitting in my ladder stand, bow hunting. I heard this gosh-awful commotion up the fencerow. I turned to see what the matter was and witnessed about 20 turkeys, young ones and mother hens, lined up and taking turns jumping up on the fence post before jumping down on the other side.

It was a quite a sight to see. Talk about organization and follow the leader! In addition, each bird would stand atop the fence pole for a second or two, as if it were playing king of the hill! Alternatively, post, in this case.

After this flock managed to relocate to my side of the fence and spread out in the alfalfa field to feed, about 30 minutes later, another flock of

15-20 arrived and executed exactly the same fence crossing exercise. I have watched old gobblers in the spring perform the post-jumping exercise many times. I guess it is a chapter in the survival manual for turkeys.

On other days, I have watched turkeys hunker down and slip under the lowest strand of barbed wire on this same fencerow. I guess some days you feel like a jump, some days you do not? What I can tell you is that checking barbed wire for turkey feathers is a good way to discover if turkeys are using that path to enter fields and pastures. Plus, if you can tell the difference between hen and gobbler feathers, you will know what brand of turkey is visiting your field.

Who says turkeys don't like to cross fences? The two flocks I watched that afternoon seem to be having fun at the fence crossing! And, I need to add, that I have seen plenty more turkeys cross fences – fly over, jump over and scoot under. If a turkey wants or needs to get to the other side of a fence, it will find a way. You can bet your sweet sarsaparilla on that.

In Henry Davis's book, he writes that turkeys are good swimmers, too. Davis hunted wild birds in the low country of South Carolina amidst the swamps, freshets and cypress trees. Many a turkey eluded Mr. Davis by jumping in the swamp and swimming away. Especially ones that were wounded and could not fly.

Yep, my mentor, Art Kibbe reminds us that "the only thing predictable about a wild turkey is that they are unpredictable."

And, I would add that wild turkeys will do anything they need to do to stay alive and well. ↓↓

Chris Young calls this photograph, "Impress the Girls" and took it in Cass County, Illinois. Photograph courtesy of Chris Young and the Springfield State Journal Register.

Chapter Twelve

"Win Without a Fight"
Run and gun vs. sit and wait

Centuries ago, Sun Tzu offered this morsel of wisdom in his classic tome, *The Art of War*. "The best strategy in war is to win without a fight." The best strategy in turkey hunting is, in my humble opinion, to win without a fight – that is, to sit and wait.

If you are in a good spot, and that is the key ingredient, then you are best off sitting and waiting for a gobbler to show up. Sooner or later, it will. Mark my word. **IF you are in a good spot.** And, IF you any kind of turkey hunter, one worth your weight in Quaker Boy Split Quads, you should know if your spot is good right off the bat, from the get-go.

IF you are sitting in a spot, say on the edge of a field or in the open woods, and you have not seen any fresh turkey sign or seen or heard the real McCoys, you are wasting your time and mine. On the other hand, IF you are cozy in your ground blind, hidden in the brush, and the corn stubble field is full of turkey tracks, droppings, feathers AND you have seen birds in this field most every day, THEN sit and wait. Do not go on a hike to find the birds. They will find you. Trust me. You are where they want to be. You are at the grocery store and they will come shopping. Because, it is all about groceries.

If you are hunting in the spring, the hens do most of the shopping and the gobblers will tag along. If it is in the fall, flocks of hens, young birds and gobblers will visit the store. Wild turkeys spend most of their awake time eating. Hello!

So hide and sit tight. Call every 15 to 20 minutes, then take a nap, read a book or count the stitches in the blind roof, if you use a pop-up blind. Sooner or later, a fat old gobbler will visit. Hens and young gobblers will visit, too. Along with all sorts and conditions of wild critters. You will not get bored because you are out in the woods, enjoying peace and quiet, finally. Leave the damn cell phone in the truck. You are NOT that important.

I am reminded of an escapade I once survived long ago. I hiked up Mt. Mitchell, which is the highest peak east of the Mississippi

River. Mount Mitchell is part of the Black Mountain range in western North Carolina. It is 6,000 odd feet above sea level and it took me three days to make the trek.

We began our ascent from the Toe River valley below and hiked to the Deep Gap trail shelter the first day. Several preachers of the Baptist persuasion and two more Episcopal parsons accompanied me. Naturally, one of my Anglican compadres toted a flask of Scotch, single malt, in his backpack. Purely for medicinal purposes, snake bites, mind you. Anglicans are permitted to imbibe in libation in moderation. First Timothy 4:23. When we finally reached Deep Gap, Tom liberated the Scotch from his pack and shared his marvelous elixir with Joe and me. I can remember it as if it were only yesterday. That double snort of Scotch neat took the edge off a killer hike and it soothed my burning leg and back muscles.

At first, the scowls of condemnation from our dry brethren heaped hills of scorn, then fire and brimstone, upon our heads. Yes, we were definitely going to Hell, but the Scotch would make the journey a bit more tolerable if we were to depart soon. But later, one by one, the tee-totalers slipped over and asked if they too could take a nip or two, for medicinal purposes, of course. We were, after all, about 2500 feet above sea level and thoroughly surrounded by backwoods and wilderness. Jim Casada calls this territory, "the back of beyond". No one would know a thing. Not even now because I have not named names.

However, that is not the point of my story. The message is that all along the trek, my companions would ask our trail leader if "we were there yet?" Moreover, they would repeat that question a hundred times, each and every day, until we finally arrived at the top. On the other hand, I quickly realized that we were "there" the moment we left our vehicles in the parking lot by the river and began our ascent. "There" was the forest, the wilderness, the wandering and the journey, from start to finish.

I will say the same thing of the turkey hunt. From the moment you leave your vehicle, hike into the woods and sit down, you are there. You are hunting. No phone calls, business meetings, difficult customers, bosses, employees, etc. You have been given the special gift of solitude and the least you can do is sit and appreciate it.

The late Benedictine monk, Thomas Merton, once wrote that the worst sin in the world is the sin of "busyness". If we spend all of our time filling it up with business and being busy, we will have no room for God. Merton suggested that we empty up some time in our lives and let God fill it. I concur. Empty time waiting for turkeys to show up, usually gets filled with all sorts of refreshing things. Even God. But, do not quote me on this!

I once taught an adult Bible Study class on the subject of spirituality and included many examples of hermits, nature lovers, anchorites and such, throughout church history. I reminded the class that Aristotle suggested that natural laws governed the universe. Along came St. Thomas Aquinas, many centuries later, and he believed that, since God had created the universe, He had created natural laws. Thus, human beings could deduce the existence of God and His actions upon the world through universal laws and observing nature.

Since no good deed goes unpunished, and I am the poster child, a rather dowdy old lady confronted me on this point.

"You mean to tell me, Parson," she huffed, "that my husband can worship God on the golf course instead of being in church on Sunday!"

"Actually no," I meekly replied. I was after all a very young parson in those days. "At least, not the way I play golf."

I was tempted to remind the lady that the Scots had invented golf and they were heavily into original sin and Calvin. The lady's husband was probably getting more religion on the golf course than in church on Sunday, especially if he played golf as poorly as I did. But, I held my tongue. I was in deep enough trouble already. No use casting any more pearls that day.

Back to turkey hunting. The longer you sit and wait, IF you are in a good spot, the sooner a big old gobbler will come and visit. If you get up and move, nine times out of ten, you will leave the woods empty-handed. Most of the time, the turkeys know you are there the moment you arrive. They have heard your truck and/or seen the headlights. They have heard you crunching through the leaves and probably have seen you without you seeing them. The trick is to fade into the background and be quiet. Remember my chapter on intrusion and fluidity? I was not kidding. The turkeys will forget about you in due time and get on with their business. Eating, mating in the spring and staying alive.

When I was young, short of tooth, long of breath, slight of build and heavy on stupid – I fell out of the stupid tree and hit every limb on the way down - I spent far too many hours cruising the woods, chasing after turkeys and spooking every critter into the next county. Nine times out of ten, the turkeys saw or heard me before I ever saw or heard them. Naturally, they ignored my calls and vacated the premises before I knew what had transpired.

One minute the woods were full of gobbles and yelps. The next minute silence. Nothing. I was none the wiser. The joke was on me.

I remember the first time Art Kibbe and I hunted in Missouri at Tony Knight's farm. The first morning we hit the woods, we did not know what to do. There were 453 million turkeys gobbling from all directions at first light and we could not decide which one to hunt. We were totally bamboozled, buffaloed and otherwise stupefied. In hindsight, we should have sat down, stayed still, called when we could get a call in between the gobble fest and waited.

Instead, we moved and moved and moved. While we chased other birds up and down the rolling hills, various and sundry gobblers would announce their arrival at our last set-up spots. Finally, we smelled the coffee, broke the code and got the picture. We found a luxurious creek bottom, spacious and green, and we sat down and hid in a dead blow down. Before long, a fat young gobbler arrived and Art dispatched it.

Henry Davis wrote in that classic turkey tome of yesteryear, *The American Wild Turkey*, that a successful turkey hunter is the turkey hunter who can sit and wait, all day, if he has to. Davis recommended that, after the hunter called and heard turkeys respond, he build a formidable blind, move in, sit still and wait. Wait as long as it took to get the birds to visit.

Long before I had read Davis's book, I had figured out that the best way to kill a decent turkey was to sit and wait.

I recall my first opening day of bow season in the fall in Illinois. I sat in my Wal-Mart folding camo chair, hidden in the brush on the edge of an alfalfa field, ALL day long. From sun up to sun down. I had one hen decoy staked in the ground at 20 yards as a distance marker. Deer, turkeys, coons, possums, foxes, coyotes and other various and sundry critters visited me all day long. I could have shot several turkeys that day, hens and young gobblers, but I waited for an old gobbler that I could call into range. Alas, they too showed up but would not get close enough for a shot.

Towards evening, I had two hungry coyotes sneak out of the woods and put the stalk on my decoy. I could have shot one of them with the bow but they got wind of me and dashed back into the trees. I came home without a tag around a turkey leg but I was refreshed, rested, invigorated and ready to go again. It beat the heck out of the best day at my office.

Today's turkey hunter can still successfully hunt Davis-style – make a blind out of natural material by snipping leafy limbs and stabbing them into the ground. And, piling up dead limbs of various and sundry sizes. To date, I have natural blinds scattered over 10 different states. I have killed gobblers out of all of them on many occasions. A good natural blind is like wine. It gets better with age.

Over the years, Art has built several log blinds in Gobbler Corner on his farm in Chautauqua County. They are strategically placed on both sides of the creek, which divides the Corner in two. Art, his son, Dan and I have spent many a splendid morning sitting in those blinds and watching the turkeys fly down and congregate. More often than not, the birds would gather around an old hen and she would lead them off in a different direction. But, every now and then, a big old gobbler would come to the call and end up in Art's garage, dangling from the scales.

At my old hunt club lease in Cass County, Illinois, John Henry still maintains the "throw up" (literally) blind during spring and fall turkey season. It is a two-man ground blind, built from dead limbs, branches and logs. The blind is now part of the natural order of things. He also has a hunt lease in Christian County, where he uses a pop-up blind. Of all of my turkey hunting "students" John Henry, next to Doc Lucky, of course has progressed to the level of master hunter.

I had two terrific natural blinds in the Back Valley at Rose Brook Farm in Missouri, of which I have written, and long to visit them once again. Perhaps, next spring I will venture west and inhabit one of my blinds. By now, it will have mellowed, aged and become a permanent part of the natural order of life in the Back Valley.

If for some reason, the blinds are gone, no problem. I will tote my Eastman blind, pop it up and settle in. Add a thermos of coffee, a good spy novel and a comfortable folding chair and I will be good-to-go, all day long!

One more tidbit. Sun time. It was the last day of the Illinois season and I had journeyed to the Upper 125 farm to tangle one more time with the last old gobbler that had survived from the original team of four brothers. Doc Lucky and I had double dispatched the first two brothers on opening day. My son-in-law, Brock Butcher, had bumped off Number Three, leaving Number Four about as lonesome as the late entertainer, "Lonesome" George Goble.

For some reason I had left home without my wrist watch and did not realize this omission until I was sitting in my natural ground blind adjacent to the little lower pasture next to the creek. At first, I panicked. Holy Cow! How am I going to tell when it is time to stop hunting, which was 1 p.m. in Illinois? Do I go home, get the watch and waste two hours? Or do I just sit, relax and rely on the sun?

Since I have spent many years outdoors, hunting, fishing, hiking and camping with the Scouts and so forth, I figured the sun would let me know when it was time to quit.

Well, I tangled with that old gobbler all morning, off and on, but it would not get close enough for a shot. I kept an eye on the sun and when I calculated it was time to quit, I headed back to the Jeep.

Wouldn't you know it, the Jeep radio clock showed it was 1 p.m. There you go. I rest my case.

Natural blinds. Natural time. Ain't nothing wrong with going natural.

The thought occurred to me. Is it legal to hunt turkeys, in the nude? If I am sitting in my blind, minding my own business, who would know? ↓↓

Chapter Thirteen

"One Below"
The Trigger Finger Rule

It is fitting, appropriate and ironic that I should end this third book in the Tailfeather Trilogy with a chapter on waterfowl hunting. If the reader recalls, the first chapter of my first book, *Bend Over Shake A Tailfeather!*, featured a solemn promise that I would give up duck hunting and only hunt turkeys. So why am I still hunting ducks? And geese?

The answer is simple. My oldest son makes me do it.

My oldest son. To whom I introduced the fine and pleasant misery of duck and goose hunting at the tender age of ten. It is he, who bears the full responsibility and blame for my renegments, retrogressions and transgressions.

For some strange and insipid reason, this thirty-something progeny has a fire in his belly for waterfowl. He hunts deer with bow and rifle. He hunts quail and pheasant in arctic temperatures. He hunts turkeys, too, having killed two of the four grand slam species so far. He dispatched the largest tom on Ft. Hood during the 2005 season, after he returned from a long and dangerous deployment in Iraq.

However, it is waterfowl that floats his decoys, cockles his cammies, tickles his fancy and otherwise makes him a satisfied soldier.

Forsooth, it was not unusual for me to volunteer to go goose hunting with him over the 2007 Christmas holidays, while he is stationed at Ft. Leavenworth, Kansas. We had shared many great duck hunts in Texas over the holidays, when he was posted at Ft. Hood with the First Cavalry Division. A great goose hunt in Kansas would be tolerable, if not semi-enjoyable.

Hello? Hit me in the head with a hammer. What was I thinking? There is no such thing as an enjoyable duck hunt.

You might recall that I have used the term, "boondoggle," a time or two, to describe hunts, especially with my late brother-in-law, Big Doug that have gone awry, headed south and otherwise left me injured, wounded and incapacitated. Not to mention, wet, cold, hypothermic, hungry, lost, clueless, broke and gameless. In all fairness to Big Doug, the mantle of doggle and the curse of boon have passed on to his nephew. With a new twist.

A boondoggle, with a new twist, is any hunt that includes waterfowl, sub-zero weather, ice, snow, coyotes and absolutely whatsoever no ducks or geese showing up. It also includes what comedians and magicians call, "a set up".

The "set up" was a series of pre-hunt phone calls proclaiming that hunt conditions were optimum; ducks and geese were covering the sky by the thousands, blotting out the sun and ripe for the taking. This set up left the father, against his better judgment, anxiously anticipating a two-day cross-country trip via pickup truck through ice and snowstorms just to shoot a greasy duck or goose or two in a new state. It was embellished with the memory of palatable ducks hunts on the Lampassas River and Stillwell Reservoir in the Texas hill country. Toss in a precocious four-year-old grand son for home entertainment and the old man was on his way, long underwear, insulated coveralls, Gore-Tex gloves and heavy quad parka packed in the suitcase.

Furthermore, and most importantly, the set up always includes a solemn promise and unspoken agreement that the "Trigger Finger" rule still applies and is in full force.

The Trigger Finger rule originated many years ago, back when the Major was a brand-new Captain and attending Captain's career course at Ft. Knox, Kentucky. One evening, the Captain called me and proposed that we meet in southern Illinois, the true goose hunting capital of the country, and go hunting. He even sweetened the pot and promised to pay for everything.

I told him that such a hunt might be a good idea and I would think about it. However, I stipulated that he would have to find a good place to go and make all of the arrangements from start to finish.

Furthermore, I added one last rock solid stipulation, the deal breaker, to the proposed goose hunt. I told my son in no uncertain terms that the only thing I was willing to do on this proposed hunt was pull the trigger. If I were to go, I wanted a goose hunt where the outfitter did everything – food, guide, decoys, heated blind – the whole kit and caboodle. The only thing I would do was exercise my trigger finger. Hence, I invented the Trigger Finger Rule with the sincere expectation that the future waterfowl event would not transpire or otherwise rear its ugly head.

After I hung up the phone, I figured that our goose hunt conversation would be the last one on the subject. And, I was quite content, satisfied, to leave things that way. I was a turkey hunter now. My waterfowl days were long past and I shoved the painful memories to the back of my mind. I really did not want to hunt geese in southern Illinois. To the best of my recollection, and up to this point in time, I had kept my promise and had not hunted waterfowl for many, many years. Period.

During this period of waterfowl abstinence, there were just a couple of quick woody hunts with the boys and Uncle Doug during a few Christmas holidays back in North Carolina but they did not really count. These hunts did not include working gobs of decoys, wading in icy water, bracing against bone-chilling wind or actually seeing any ducks. We just tagged along with Doug and his buddy, Wayne, and listened to wood ducks zip through the air at tree top level in the morning darkness. Hardly a shot was ever fired. Within a matter of minutes, Doug would proclaim that the hunt was over and it was time for breakfast. These "hunts" were more like bird watching and did not count.

Well, a couple of days later, the Captain phoned again to inform me that he had made a reservation for us to hunt at Crab Orchard Goose Club in Marion, Illinois. He would take care of all the arrangements – motel, club and guide – the whole shooting match. All I had to do, he reminded me, was exercise my trigger finger. He would handle everything else.

This sounded too good to be true. But, I also knew not to underestimate the leadership of an officer in our nation's Army.

We met in Marion on the appointed Friday evening at the appointed motel. The motel had reserved a very nice room and the Captain paid for it! Now this was a pleasant surprise and greased the wheels, which were now rolling downhill towards a real waterfowl hunt. The Captain also paid for supper and the hunt fees the next day. At this point, I was beginning to think that all I would have to do is pull the trigger. I also began to scheme of other opportunities, which included turkeys and not waterfowl, that I might conjure up to separate him from his hard-earned cash.

Dark and early the next morning, he drove me out to the hunt club, where we checked in. The manager assigned us a pit blind and a guide, a pleasant enough middle-aged fellow who was also a deputy sheriff. After a continental breakfast of hot coffee and assorted rolls and doughnuts – no Little Debbies were on the menu - my son carried my shotgun and shell bag, along with his, to the hunt club Suburban and we saddled up for a heated ride to the corn field and pit blind. *So far, so good,* I thought. *But, the jury was still out.*

When we arrived at the blind, we proceeded to climb into a rather large and roomy concrete pit blind, equipped with a large and toasty gas heater, running full blast. Surrounding the blind were several hundred Canada goose decoys in excellent condition and well spread. I was beginning to think that we might just shoot a goose.

We settled into our deluxe accommodations, all warm and toasty, and waited for the first flights of geese to depart Crab

Orchard reservoir and head for our field and groceries. My son even offered to load my gun, but I told him thanks, but no thanks. I would make an exception to the Rule and slip the shells into the chamber using two fingers.

Before long, the first long V of geese appeared on the horizon. Behind it was formation after formation as far as the eye could see. The geese turned and zeroed in on our location. Our guide called a time or two and sounded pitiful. I could call a darn sight better than he could without a call. But, since I had invoked the "Trigger Finger" rule, I had left my goose calls at home in the top dresser drawer, where a great deal of retired junk resided. At this point, I had an inkling that we were in trouble.

The first flock of geese glided over our blind, wings cupped and well within gun range. But our guide did not call for a shot. The geese passed over and finished further down in the field. A barrage of shots announced their arrival and subsequent demise.

No problem, I thought. *More geese were on the way and we would get a shot soon.*

The next flock passed overhead, again in range, but continued on unmolested. Again, the guide did not call for a shot. Another flock arrived and sailed safely over our heads. For two solid hours, every goose in southern Illinois flew over our blind in range! The guide continued to hold off our shots while hundreds of geese dropped to the field behind us. Every blind behind us opened up and blasted their limit of geese. We just watched. Shotless. Frustrated. And pissed off.

If memory serves me well, at some point in this debacle, our guide let it slip out that he was under orders to let the geese pass over us so that they would finish in front of the other blinds behind us. At this point, I glared at the idiot and informed him that the Captain had paid our fees and we were due shots, too. And, he had better do something about the situation. ASAP.

The deputy sheriff-pseudo goose guide got the message, loud and clear, and realized that his financial tip at the end of the day was in serious jeopardy. He also probably deduced that he might finish the day with a broken nose or black eye since I was considering exercising the "Five Finger" Rule – a fist. Followed by a goose call crammed up a significant bodily orifice of my choosing. When it became painfully apparent that we had had enough of this crap, the guide whipped out his walkie-talkie and called for backup.

Soon the club Suburban arrived and transported us to another field and another blind. The club owner heaped apologies upon us for the lousy hunt so far, but, at this point, we were not inclined to respond kindly. I could smell a rat and was inclined to tell the sorry SOBs where they could go, demand my son's money back and request a speedy departure from the premises. But, out of respect for my son, discretion being the better part of valor and Uncas being the last Mohican, I held my tongue, swallowed my anger and backed off.

We arrived at the new blind, after lunch, unloaded our gear and hunkered down in our hole in the ground. At this point, and since I chose not to share my "true feelings" with the management, I vividly remember that empty feeling of despair, born long ago on my first hapless duck hunt and nurtured by years of waterfowl foul-ups, swell in the deep recesses of my gut and sweep over me, a dark pall of impending disaster. We were totally "boondoggled" with no hope of rescue.

We spent the rest of the day in the new blind, watching the same old geese avoid our set up, finish in front of other blinds and hunters, collapse and fall to the earth and die. The guide's feeble attempts at calling added insult to injury. The hunt finally and mercifully ended.

Forsooth, the Captain and I were the only goose hunters that day that did not shoot a goose. Everyone else, including their guides, shot their limit and posed for pictures, dead geese dangling above their heads, from the dead goose rack at the lodge. The Captain did manage to bust two hulls at a goose that appeared in range. But, it was not and he missed. I, on the other hand, did not exercise my trigger finger. Not once. It hung limp and lonely next to its buddy, the Middle Finger. Which I almost exercised later, when the guide sheepishly mentioned a customary tip at the end of the hunt.

Needless to say, that was our first and last Canada goose hunt at Crab Orchard. We did visit the Crab a month later for the special light goose conservation season and shot a bunch of snows and blues, after a long and hasty drive down to Cairo. However, that hunt was too little, too late and did little to compensate for the previous misery. At least our guide, the Cowboy, knew what the heck he was doing on that day and retrieved all of our dead geese.

Moreover, I should add, that I was pleasantly pleased to read an advertisement in a recent edition of the Ducks Unlimited magazine, while waiting in the dentist's office. The ad announced that Crab Orchard was for sale. Later that month, we passed right by the Crab in Marion, on the way to Kansas and the Christmas Eve goose hunt. You can see the Crab from the highway. I slowed down and took a good look at the place. Weeds covered its cornfields. The goose ponds were dried up and gone. The clubhouse was boarded up and stood empty on the hilltop. The dead goose rack was history. Crab Orchard was out of business. I, for one, did not mourn the loss.

We arrived in Kansas City later on that very same day, in the middle of an ice and snowstorm. Traffic slowed to a crawl about 30 miles outside of the city and those who chose to ignore the conditions slid off the highway, careened into one another and otherwise paid the price for their stupidity. We, on the other hand, slowed way down and crept our way to Ft. Leavenworth. We arrived tired and stressed but safe.

The storm ended that night and the next day the Major took me to visit Cabela's in Kansas City to buy him a new layout blind for Christmas and non-resident hunting license for me. We spent the rest of the afternoon shopping for Christmas presents for the family. I bought my wife a lovely snowflake necklace in memory of our horrible trip into the city.

After a good night's rest, I awoke the next morning and proceeded to put on every stitch of hunting clothing I had. I met my son in the kitchen, where he planted a fresh, hot cup of coffee into my hands and then told me to saddle up. I followed his orders and we left the house in the frigid dark Kansas morning. A foot of new snow glistened in the light of a majestic full Midwest moon. Not a good omen I mused. A full moon meant that most of the geese in the area probably had migrated south ahead of the snowstorm. Any remaining birds would have changed their feeding patterns, taking advantage of the bright moonlight.

The Chevy 4x4 truck headed down the street about one block and stopped. We picked up Scott, another Major, with whom my son served in the 1-8 Cavalry in Iraq. These two officers, their wives and children were close friends, almost family. Scott was waiting for us in the cold driveway. He hopped into the front seat of the Chevy truck, while I tried to keep warm in the back. Scott and Heath would do all the work that morning. My job was to pull the trigger on my shotgun. The Trigger Finger Rule.

After a 45-minute drive west from Ft. Leavenworth, we arrived in Jefferson County and at the fields and marshes of Perry Lake. The marsh was frozen solid. The Delaware River was frozen solid. The cornfield next to the river was covered in snow and frozen solid. The truck thermometer registered one below zero. I figured that if I stepped out of the heated truck, I would be frozen solid, too. I could smell a boondoggle in the making. From the start.

As soon as I did step out of the truck, reluctantly, my moustache froze solid and icicles formed inside my nostrils. It was indeed below zero. I had been below zero many, many times before and was not really happy to be there once again. I waddled out to the field to help the boys put a finishing touch on the layout blinds and decoy spread. Then, with my son's assistance, I crammed into the blind like a hotdog, still frozen, in a bun. I did not particularly like the idea of lying flat on the ground, with heaps of snow piled on me, but my son reminded me that the "snow had insulating qualities."

Terrific, I thought, *his house also had insulating qualities, the warm blanket on the guest bed, the benefits of central gas heating and, most importantly, indoor plumbing.*

I must admit that I did not feel any colder, tucked into the coffin blind, but the picture of a dead body lying in its casket, staring back at the ceiling, entered my mind. I told my son that I now knew how dead people felt, while lying in state. Cold and wishing they were somewhere else.

Obviously, I did not savor the new experience of lying flat on my back in a Kansas cornfield in sub-zero temperatures.

For a split second, my bladder signaled that it was ready to eliminate the early morning coffee but the thought of one below zero shut the whole system down, from top to bottom. We lay on the ground and waited for the sun to rise and the geese to arrive. My son continued to cheer me up and promise that geese would arrive soon.

He lied. The sun rose in the clear blue sky. The temperature struggle to warm up to 10 degrees, maybe even 15. However, the geese did not arrive, as promised, soon or later or at any time. Nor did any ducks. The only animals to arrive all morning were a noisy flock of turkeys, putting and clucking, at the end of the field and a rather large, hungry-looking coyote that put the sneak on our decoys and us. I suggested to my son for the tenth or twelfth time that I thought the geese had migrated south ahead of the snowstorm and with the aid of the full moon.

One thing was certain, the big prairie sky remained clear, dazzling blue and empty. The geese were gone and we were knee-deep in boondoggle.

We finally surrendered, retrieved the decoys, folded up the coffin blinds, loaded up the truck and headed for home. On the trip back, we did not see any geese for 30 miles – in the air or in the surrounding fields. We DID, however, see turkeys. Lots of turkeys. At some point, I don't remember exactly when, I suggested that we change our priorities, that we cancel the goose chase and focus on wild turkeys. The Kansas fall-winter season was still in and we could shoot up to three birds in Zone Two.

Forsooth, to make a long story short, it warmed up the day after Christmas and we returned to Perry Lake so my son could chop a big hole in the ice with an axe, toss out a couple of decoys and duck hunt. On this outing, we took Tim, another major in the Army, and an old Citadel classmate. One, obviously dumb and lost, mallard finished in our hole but Tim shot three times and missed it. We spent most of that morning watching a dozen great big Kansas gobblers feed in an open field on the other side of the marsh.

Walking back to the truck, we bumped into a large flock of 50 turkeys or more, feeding in the same cornfield where we had goose hunted a couple of days earlier. The turkeys saw us and took off. Some vanished into the woods along the riverbank. A big chunk flew across the river. We hiked over to the corner of the field to inspect the situation and discovered thousands of turkey tracks, of all sizes and shapes. Once again, I suggested that we deep six the goose-duck boondoggles and get down to serious business – turkey hunting.

After another trip to Cabela's in Kansas City to purchase turkey stamps, we returned to the same Kansas cornfield the next morning in milder weather – 20 degrees or so. On this trip, my youngest son, Ian, accompanied us. Ian is the son who has yet to shoot a turkey and prefers to fly fish for trout. He was in his final year of graduate school and drove over from St. Louis for the holidays. This time we carried Heath's large Cabela's Full Draw blind and chairs. We set the blind up in the far corner of the field, surrounded by thousands of turkey tracks, and settled inside.

At sunrise, the turkeys announced their presence across the river with a multitude of yelps and clucks. Loud yelps. Soft yelps. Coarse gobbler yelps. All kinds of clucks, boinks, cutts and happy turkey talk filled the river bottom. I joined in the calling with a short but generous invitation to come visit the cornfield and have some breakfast.

I am not sure why the birds did not accept my breakfast invitation. But, they preferred to stay on the other side of the river and feed. Every now and then, one of them would call to me and I would answer. But, it became apparent that they were not coming to the field, at least, for a while. I figured they were thinking lunch instead of breakfast. There must have been plenty of acorns where they were and had no reason to come to the field.

In the meantime, whilst we were talking turkey to the crowd across the river, another group of turkeys – 11 gobblers, to be specific – must have heard the racket and decided to head our way. On our side of the river. They announced their presence from the woods with a couple of coarse yelps. I responded in kind and about five minutes later, they arrived. In full view, they crossed the forest service road at the end of the field, one at a time, and we counted them as they appeared to be headed our way. The gobblers were about 70 yards out.

We raised our guns and anxiously assumed that they would walk down the edge of the field soon and arrive in range. Instead, they slipped into the small chunk of woods behind us, along side the frozen Delaware River, and began to putt, cutt and otherwise let us know they were not happy about something. I told the boys that something was not right, got up and unzipped the back door to the blind. I slipped out of the blind and slowly inspected the situation.

Our gobblers had walked across the frozen river and were on the other bank, only about 60 yards away, watching our side. And, the coyote that had heard our calling and followed the birds in, was putting the stalk on us. The coyote continued to slink through the trees along the bank and head straight for me. Since I had left my shotgun in the blind I stood motionless, watched and waited. By this time, my sons had joined me and the oldest had his shotgun aimed at the dog. He was ready to shoot.

"*Click!*" The safety on his 11-87 UltiMag announced our presence and the coyote spun around and sprinted off scared but untouched.

Well, I wanted to stay in the blind and wait for the turkeys across the river to come and eat lunch in the field, which I was sure they would do. But, I got out-voted by a goose hunter and fly fisherman. They decided to quit the hunt and head home instead of shooting turkeys. The wives and grandson had plans for us and we could not be late. Thus, we packed up our gear, trudged back across the field to the truck and reluctantly left the turkeys behind.

Hindsight being 20-20 and Davy being a Crockett, in my humble opinion, we should have been hunting turkeys all the while. Geese and ducks should not have been a part of the Christmas holiday hunt formula. Some simple pre-holiday research by my son, the Major, would have revealed a generous Kansas fall-winter turkey season with a three-bird limit in Zone Two. A few scouting trips to Perry Lake, even if they included lugging goose decoys, coffin blinds and not shooting geese, would have revealed the presence of copious amounts of wild turkeys ripe for the taking.

But, that is water over the dam. A moot point. One more major (pun intended) boondoggle in the history of boondoggles.

The Major phoned the other day to share another goose report. God, he will not give it up. He, Scott and some other officers traveled across the river to Missouri and went on a paid, guided goose hunt. The Major reported that he did see geese and actually shot a goose. However, a 14-year-old kid, next to him in the blind, claimed that he had shot the same bird, too. So, as I taught him long ago, my son relinquished his claim to the dead goose and returned home boondoggled one more time.

I have suggested that we visit them next Thanksgiving instead of Christmas, when the weather would be warmer. I have also added a new stipulation to the One Finger Rule. No goose or duck hunting will be allowed, permitted or otherwise discussed, considered or mentioned.

We will stay at his house; play with the new baby; duel light sabers with the grandson and otherwise act grandparently. We will also hunt wild turkeys.

Furthermore, I have added an important codicil to the family will. If he is to inherit what we do not spend before our demise – and we will try to spend it all - I must shoot at least three Kansas turkeys, preferably in the fall, before the Army transfers him to a new post. ↓↓

Chapter Fourteen

"Turkey Lounger For Sale"
No More Run & Gun For Me

The time has come for me to quit running and gunning for turkeys. It is not because I am getting too old or out of shape to get around in the woods. I still get around just fine. For a fat man approaching 60, I can hold my own against most of the young Turks with whom I hunt and teach how to turkey hunt. The fact is I am a chicken! A yellow-bellied, chicken-lizard coward. I will never again push my luck as I did this past spring, while hunting on the banks of Mulberry Creek and its swamp.

The day began with the promise of the Treehouse Gobbler showing up and giving me another shot. I had missed the sorry rascal earlier in the season and figured I had scared him clear out of the county. I was surprised and pleased to hear him gobbling in his spot over the swamp again later in the season. On that particular morning, my buddy, Terry Corder, from South Carolina, was with me as we hunkered down in one of my favorite spots at the back end of a small uncultivated field near the White Oak River.

The Treehouse Gobbler announced his presence, bright and early, and I could not help but toss a few calls in his direction, about 150 yards away, at the appropriate times. Between us were another small grassy field and an old fencerow. I did not expect the gobbler to fly down into the grassy field, seeing how I had taken a shot at him in that precise spot the week before. I figured he would rocket off the roost and fly north over to Stroud's field.

Surprisingly, at sunrise, the old gobbler left his tree and fluttered to the ground – on our side. He spent the next few minutes gobbling and strutting in the middle of the grassy field. I, in response, cranked up my calling. For a short time, it sounded as if the bird was coming closer and heading for an opening in the fencerow and into our field. However, a second adult gobbler, two Jakes and two hens showed up in the grassy field and the entourage headed west for the front end of the field and the cabbage patch, where Rudy Simione and Whip Whipper were waiting.

As luck would have it, a gobbler fight between the two old toms ensued, while the Jakes watched and the hens walked away to feed. Terry and I watched the shenanigans with our binoculars and I provided Rudy and Whip a play-by-play via our radios. They could hear the commotion but could not see the birds. The hens, on the other hand, showed little interest in the fight and slowly fed their way back east towards our end of the field. When the fight ended, the Treehouse Gobbler won and returned to strutting and gobbling. The losing tom seemed content to tag along with the winner.

Realizing that the hens had moved to the back end of the field, the gobblers, young and old, headed east. All six turkeys were now heading right for us and we began to get our hopes up. The way things were going, I figured we had a pretty good chance to get a shot and I told Terry to get ready. The hens would pass by my decoy and us first and they did. Next, the Jakes arrived and nervously lingered, almost in range. Finally, the Treehouse Gobbler, in full strut, and his new buddy showed up. Events were shaping up just fine. Terry and I raised our shotguns, aimed at the birds and prepared to shoot.

However, this is the point where I need to philosophize.

No matter how much preparation you put into your hunt; no matter how great your calling is; no matter how good your set-up and camouflage are; no matter how fired up a gobbler can get; no matter how clean your underwear is; when you hunt turkeys, you must remember that there are always circumstances, which you cannot control. Such as the sudden approach of a thunderstorm or the untimely appearance of a coyote or bobcat, stalking your turkeys. My buddy, Ron Clough, aptly says, "Roosted ain't roasted."

As the event of a gobbler coming to the gun unfolds and my heart beats faster and it looks as if I am going to shoot a turkey, a thin slice of doubt remains firmly lodged in my mind. No matter how good things are going, there are always circumstances beyond your control that can screw things up. When these circumstances don't happen and you end up shooting the gobbler, it makes the shot even more special.

Just when it looked as if we were going to get two shots at two gobblers, a double, and Terry's first longbeard, a big white spray truck, the Honey Wagon, arrived on the scene and barreled down the road along the fencerow that divided the two small fields.

I hate to say this but this was not the first time the spray truck has screwed me up. In fact, it has screwed up at least one hunt every year that I have hunted at this particular farm. I keep telling myself that I am going to find another place to hunt. But, old habits die hard and each year finds me back in the same set of circumstances. I will never learn.

Forsooth, the truck arrived at the wrong time and at the wrong place. It could not have been planned more perfectly! At first, the

Treehouse Gobbler ignored the truck and the noise and strutted almost into my shotgun range. I had a full frontal shot at this strutting tom at about 50 yards with my long-range 11-87 Eliminator. But the thought of missing the bird again combined with the silly hope that he would come closer kept me from pulling the trigger. The truck stopped on the other side of the fencerow and the Treehouse Gobbler kept strutting. I was just about to pull the trigger when, all of a sudden,

"*Bam!*" The truck door slammed shut.

It took one second for the old gobbler to break strut and bolt like a scalded dog running for the next county. Terry and I watched both adult gobblers race by us, brown blurs against the short tan grass, and disappear into the woods and swamp. In two shakes and one door slam, the game was over. Turkeys - 6 Hunters – 0.

Ten minutes later, the truck left and we spent the rest of the morning, trying to coax the birds out of the swamp and back into the field. After an hour or so, we moved to the field behind us, where my blind was set up at Bear Corner and finished the hunt there. The birds did not show up. Not a peep, not a yelp or gobble was heard. Around noon, we left my blind and headed to Norma's store with Rudy and Whip for lunch. After lunch, we decided to return to the scene of the crime. Rudy had to leave to teach a class so Whip hunkered down in my "confiscated" blind on one end of the field, near the cabbage patch, while Terry returned to our early morning spot.

I, on the other hand, made the fateful decision to walk across the field and park my skinny butt in my Gobbler Lounger near the spot where the Treehouse Gobbler had roosted that morning. Since the birds had not returned to the field so far that day, I figured they had traveled on down the creek and would return to the roost site and visit the field that evening. I sat in the brush, well hidden, on the edge of the field, with my back to Mulberry Creek and swamp.

The afternoon sun and the satisfaction of a full stomach lulled me into sleep quickly and I dozed for over an hour. After I awoke, refreshed, I perked up and began to watch and listen for turkeys. Every 20 minutes or so, I would call softly into the creek and swamp behind me. After an hour or two, I began to hear soft turkey sounds in the creek bottom and I got ready. I pulled both knees up, rested my shotgun on my left knee and pushed the safety off. Birds were close and soon would exit the swamp and enter the field near me. In a few minutes, I would get another chance at the Treehouse Gobbler.

As I sat there, alert and ready for action, I noticed with my powerful peripheral vision, which I have mentioned in a previous chapter, a long, slender object slowly slither out from under my seat and in between my legs. The long, slender object turned out to be a three-foot-long copperhead snake about three inches thick. Its pink and tan hourglass pattern was unmistakable. Instantly, I realized I was in big trouble.

In the half century that I have spent in the woods, hunting, fishing and camping, I have never ever had a poisonous snake get that close to me. I have seen many rattlesnakes, copperheads and cottonmouths and I have given them a wide berth before anything bad happened. But, to have an adult copperhead slide out from under your rear end and slowly slither between your legs is a terrible close encounter, to say the least.

The first thing I did was freeze. I did not move a muscle. I reckon it took nerves of steel to do that but I had no choice. Next, since the snake was moving away and did not appear to notice me, I started hoping that it would just keep on moving. Soon it would be far enough away that I could get up and leave. However, the snake had other ideas.

No sooner had its tail passed my boots and it looked as if it might slither away, it decided to stop, turn around, double up and rear its ugly head.

Now, close your eyes and picture this. I am sitting only about four or five inches off the ground in the Gobbler Lounger, which means I am basically on the ground and now at eye level with a poisonous snake about two feet away and at the end of my boots. The snake is too close for me to move without being bitten. The only thing I can do is move my shotgun slowly, inch by inch, until the muzzle is directly in front of the snake's head and pull the trigger. All the while, the snake is reared up and watching me.

Well, I proceeded to do just that. Although it felt like ten minutes, it probably took ten seconds for me slowly to move my shotgun off my left knee, to the right and into position without the snake striking back. Once in position, I pulled the trigger and the snake's head evaporated into thin air. I jumped up at once and shouted at the top of my lungs, "Holy S—t!"

Unfortunately, the turkeys behind me heard the commotion and headed back down the creek. I really did not care. My hunting friends also heard the uproar. I picked up my seat, vest, and got the heck out of Dodge.

Both Whip and Terry called me on my cell phone to see if I had shot the Treehouse Gobbler. I informed them that a three-foot copperhead had died instead and that I was too upset to tell them the whole story on the phone. I would fill them in later at the truck.

So now you know the whole story and the reason why I have a Gobbler Lounger for sale, cheap. Although it is a very comfortable seat, probably the most comfortable one that I have ever used, I will never, ever use it again as long as I live.

I will never ever sit on the ground or near the ground again while turkey hunting.

Never. And, you can take that to the bank.

I went turkey hunting a couple of days later at Tee Tallman's farm and sat the whole morning in my folding chair, well-hidden in the bushes on the edge of a food plot and three feet above the ground.

From now on, I will sit in my chair, in my blind, and mind my own business. No more running and gunning, especially around creeks and swamps, for me.

I have learned my lesson well. ↓↓

The author, second from left, shot his Illinois longbeard on the last day of his Brown County hunt. It took two hours of calling to this bird but it finally appeared. Doc's Double Bull blind and a full size chair made the wait comfortable and easy. Best of all, no snakes were present.

Bill and his favorite author, Tom Kelly, at the 2007 NWTF Convention in Nashville, TN. Photography by Bob Gowen.

TurkeyHuntBooks.Com

Tailfeather Press - Purveyors of Distinctive Books on Wild Turkey Hunting

Bend Over Shake A Tailfeather!

Thirteen chapters, 183 pages. This perfect bound book is a favorite amongst readers far and wide, young and old. It features entertaining stories of foolishness gleaned from trips around the country while pursuing that brassy bird of bodaciousness, the wild turkey. Bill weaves a tapestry of 20-plus years of turkey hunting with silver-gray threads of wit, charm and self-deprecation. The book is filled with humor, homespun philosophy, satire and zany zingers. You will enjoy every page. Price: $15.95

Bend Over Here It Comes!

Bill bags a double beard with this one! Another 13 chapters, 197 pages, of whacky and wild misadventures while chasing more wild turkeys around the country. Chapters include offbeat and screwball topics such as "turkey wives," "excuses," "gizmos and gadgets" to name a few. Let's face it; the life of a turkey hunter is filled with madness, mania and mental challenges. Privette plugs the hole, fills the gap and otherwise provides the absolute proof that folks who hunt wild turkeys are a special breed. Bill claims he was kicked out of his family tree, bounced over to the stupid tree and hit every limb on the way down. Order the book and find out if you are related! Price: $15.95

First Edition Bend Over Shake A Tailfeather! 2005

We published the "Little Book" in the fall of 2005 for friends and family. It was a fun project and a dry run for the new publishing business. Since then, the Little Book has become an important item amongst turkey book collectors. We printed 500 and signed and numbered them. The book also includes a First Edition page. Since it was intended for a small audience, it is unabridged. You will not find this book for sale in retail stores or at Amazon.Com. We have some copies left. Price: $34.95

CD: Shake A Tailfeather, Part One 2006

The author tells his favorite stories from his first two books. It features 80 minutes of tall tales and tom foolery while hunting wild turkeys. The CD is free with book orders or can be purchased separately for $9.95

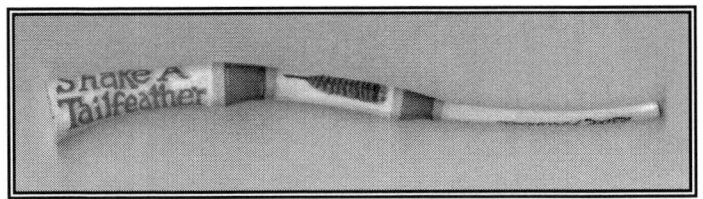

Wing Bone Calls

Bill makes special wing bone calls for his hunting buddies. He signs and numbers them, too. He makes two- and three-piece calls with colorful custom joint wrappings and art work. Please visit **TurkeyHuntBooks.Com** for more information on ordering a special wing bone call.

Box Calls

Bill makes custom box calls for his hunting buddies. Made from mahogany and walnut, one at a time, they are signed, numbered and feature special inlay work. His special presentation calls are not for sale. However, he is considering making and selling a standard box call for the general public. Visit **TurkeyHuntBooks.Com** for the announcement, availability and price of the standard calls.

Decals

We sell custom turkey track decals and will be adding a decal page to the website soon. Our decals are a special automotive grade and long lasting. Colors are gold and sparkle green. Price: $10.95 for four tracks.

TurkeyHuntBooks.Com Direct Order Form

Photocopy this form. Enclose check or credit card info. Mail to: Tailfeather Press, 1119 Hendricks Ave., Jacksonville, NC 28540. Phone orders: 910.455.5713. Make checks out to Tailfeather Press.

Name: _____

Address: _____

City: _____ State: _____

Zip Code: _____

Item	Price	Quantity
Shake A Tailfeather One More Time! Signed.	$20.95	
Shake A Tailfeather One More Time! Signed and numbered.	$25.95	
Bend Over Here It Comes! Signed and Numbered	$24.95	
Bend Over Here It Comes! Signed.	$15.95	
Bend Over Shake A Tailfeather! Signed.	$15.95	
Bend Over Shake A Tailfeather! First Edition Unabridged Limited numbered and signed copies	$34.95	
Tailfeathers Part One Audio CD Free with book order, otherwise:	$9.95	

Shipping: $4.00 for first book, add $1 for each additional book.

NC residents add 6.75% sales tax

Total Due:

Credit Card Orders

Card Holder's address should match above shipping address for card approval.

Visa or MasterCard Number: _____

CID # (3 digit# on back of card): _____

Expiration Date: _____